S0-BNE-455

THE ROLLING STONES REVEALED

Copyright © 2007 The Foundry Creative Media Company Ltd

This edition published by World Publications Group, Inc.
by arrangement with The Foundry Creative Media Company Ltd.

World Publications Group, Inc.
140 Laurel Street
East Bridgewater, MA 02333
www.wrldpub.com

Publisher and Creative Director: Nick Wells
Project Editors: Sara Robson and Polly Willis
Picture Research: Gemma Walters
Designer: Mike Spender
Production: Chris Herbert and Claire Walker

All rights reserved. No part of this publication may be reproduced, stored in a retrieval system or transmitted in any form or by any means, electronic, mechanical, photocopying, recording or otherwise, without the prior permission of the publisher.

PICTURE CREDITS: Foundry Arts: 18(l), 23(r), 25(b), 27(b), 33(r), 36(r), 41(l), 44 (t), 47(r), 49(b), 64(t), 71(r), 72(b), 79(l), 80(l), 86(l), 96(l), 99(t), 104(l), 108(t), 116(t), 118(b), 125(b), 131(r), 134(l), 140(l), 143(b), 147(l), 148(r), 150(r), 152(r), 156(r), 165(l), 166(r), 172(r), 191(r), 195(b).

With grateful thanks to **Redferns** and the following list of photographers: Richard E. Aaron: 125, 127, 128–9, 132, 133, 168; Jorgen Angel: 108, 109; BBC Photo Library: 18–9, 25, 94–5, 95–6; Paul Bergen: 172, 174–5, 186–7, 188; Amber Books: 82; George Chin: 153; Rogan Coles: 165; Fin Costello: 116; Grant Davis: 193; Phil Dent: 163; Ian Dickson: 118; David Farrell: 13; Peter Francis: 26; GAB Archives: 30, 35, 39, 63, 65, 73, 88, 92, 117, 119, 124, 126, 136, 146, 151, 157, 169, 173, 182; Harry Goodwin: 32–3, 98; Tom Hanley: 78; John Hopkins: 12; Ron Howard: 42–3, 91, 100; Mick Hutson: 171, 189, 190–1; K&K Ulf Kruger OHG: 44; Ivan Keeman: 46–7; Dennis King: 29; Robert Knight: 99, 104–5, 114; Michel Linssen: 167; Andrew Maclear: 70–1, 74; Michael Ochs Archive: 15, 16, 31, 38, 41, 62, 64, 68, 69, 72, 75, 80–1, 83, 85, 89, 90, 115, 121; Keith Morris: 149; Bernd Muller: 170, 176–7, 184–5; Jan Olofsson: 60–1; Peter Pakvis: 194; Don Paulsen: 24, 34, 40, 49, 86–7; Jan Persson: 86–7; Stefan M. Prager: 195; Andrew Putler: 120; RB: 20; David Redfern: 21, 27, 37, 55, 76, 84; Ebet Roberts: 140, 142, 143, 147, 148, 152, 154, 156, 158–9; Peter Saunders: 77, 79; Diana Scrimgeour: 179, 196–7; Robert Verhorst: 141, 150, 166; Robert Vincett: 17; David Warner Ellis: 110–1; Val Wilmer: 14; Graham Wiltshire: 93, 106, 107, 122–3, 134–5, 155, 162, 178.

Topham Picturepoint: 22–3, 28, 36, 45, 48, 50, 51, 52, 53, 54, 56–7, 58, 59, 112, 113, 130–1, 137, 144–5, 160–1, 164, 183.

JASON DRAPER (author) comes from Plymouth and currently lives in London. He is the Reviews Editor at *Record Collector*, the monthly music magazine dedicated to collecting music of all genres and on all formats. He has written for *Uncut*, *Metal Hammer*, *Sound Nation*, *Big Issue Cymru* and *Buzz* magazines, and was a contributor to Flame Tree's *Definitive Illustrated Encyclopedia of Rock* (2006).

He would like to thank mum, dad, Kirsty, Jake, Joel, Jack, Tim and Alan.

ISBN: 978 1 57215 879 5

Printed and bound in China

11 13 15 14 12

1 3 5 7 9 10 8 6 4 2

THE ROLLING STONES REVEALED

TEXT BY JASON DRAPER
INTRODUCTION BY PAUL DU NOYER

JG PRESS

CONTENTS

1973-81 — 102

1982-99 — 138

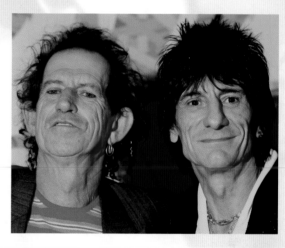

2000-PRESENT — 180

INDEX — 198

INTRODUCTION

I'm having lunch in a Chelsea restaurant with a sprightly gent of 60-plus. His wits are quick and he's a fabulous source of softly spoken gossip. He reflects a moment on one especially key evening in his life, early in 1963. 'If you're not sure who rock'n'roll belongs to,' says Andrew Loog Oldham, 'then it surely isn't you.'

When Oldham was 19 and London's sharpest young hustler, he clapped eyes on The Rolling Stones at a backroom blues gig in a suburban boozer. And that night he glimpsed a band who – with a little help and a lot of hype – really might claim rock'n'roll as their own. He was, of course, proved right beyond his wildest calculations. Within six years they were playing to vast, awe-struck multitudes and being billed – without the least fear of contradiction – as 'the greatest rock'n'roll band in the world'.

The Rolling Stones are the irreducible essence of rock music, and their astonishing story has not yet finished. Oldham's first sighting was the start of his managerial career with the Stones and effectively the night they achieved lift-off. In four years they rose, and for the past 40 years they've declined to fall. During their journey they've been almost everything that rock'n'roll has represented, from bratty rebellion to corporate respectability. They were never meant to last this long, but as Keith Richards once revealed: 'I have still not discovered all the myriad possibilities of "Midnight Rambler" or "Satisfaction" ... I could play "Jumpin' Jack Flash" all night if my hand would bear it.'

They took rock music, and the culture it inspired into being, to unexplored extremes. Some have gone further since: among The Sex Pistols, Kiss, Mötley Crüe and the rest there are bands who have caused more scandals, looked more shocking, taken more drugs, despoiled more virgins or whatever. But the Stones did so many of these things first, or so memorably, or with such inimitable panache, that the others were merely tracing their footsteps. Except, of course, that most who tried following in the Stones' footprints got lost along the way, to end up in the abyss of oblivion or self-destruction – which the Stones, so cannily, never did. With one exception, they wound up rich and settled, in some cases happily married, in Jagger's case a knight of the realm, and in Keith's a walking defiance of medical science.

Thanks to their fallen star, hell's cherub Brian Jones, the Stones became symbols of crash-and-burn mortality but also of survival against the odds. Thus they embody both sides of the rock'n'roll myth. In the shadowy demise of Jones, in the shuddering menace of their darkest songs and in the disaster of Altamont, The Rolling Stones can encompass death and apocalypse – and yet, as everyone of us who loves their music can testify, they are a supremely life-affirming experience.

At Altamont they broke the unspoken contract that rock stars have always had with their audience – namely that all this danger and

rebellion, this dressing up and looking savage, is really just a big game of pretend and nobody gets hurt. Only this time, somebody did. Commentators have always made much of Altamont's symbolic end to the hippie dream and they are right. The 1960s crashed to a close that day and the next decade would evolve a pop culture underscored by glamour, decadence, anger and fatigue. The Stones were innocent of the madness that swirled around them, but their music was already, and brilliantly, incorporating a brutal knowledge that no other act, with the possible exception of Dylan, ever came close to nailing.

Immortal as their greatest songs may be, the live arena is still the heart of The Rolling Stones' existence. By the early 1970s bands like Led Zeppelin and The Grateful Dead had dramatically remodelled our expectations of a rock show. The four-songs-and-off routine of the package tours gave way to gargantuan sets with sprawling solos and phenomenal volume. Aesthetics and equipment developed in tandem and the Stones seized the moment. Here at last was their opportunity to surpass The Beatles, who split in 1970 and stopped touring four years before

that, demoralized by the inadequacies of 1960s technology. The Rolling Stones were never such masters of the studio as their rivals, but they were a sinuous and funky blues band, with the capacity to stretch to their full size on a stage. Thus they became, just as their magnificently arrogant slogan proclaimed, the greatest rock'n'roll band in the world.

Even today The Rolling Stones are innovators in live performance, vying with younger competitors such as U2 in discovering just how much can now be done with video technology and stage design, even before the most colossal audiences. Keith and Charlie would prefer it if we admired the Stones for pure musicianship, but Jagger is smart enough to know that skill and riffs alone will not keep their show on the road. Latterday albums like *Voodoo Lounge* and *Bridges To Babylon* were conceived as visual spectaculars before they were composed as music. Add the potent allure of witnessing living history, and the Stones' appeal is complete. To many these days a new Rolling Stones album is unimportant – but to see them play is an obligation. It's literally something that everyone should do at least once in their lifetime.

Sometimes on that stage the players can look almost a mile apart, yet they play with the same intensity as the band that jammed in claustrophobic London pubs, their empathy now heightened to telepathic levels by the decades of musical comradeship. Forget his Satanic decadence, it's Jagger's legendary athleticism – he's the son of a physical fitness instructor, after all – that conquers the wide-open spaces. Charlie Watts no longer pounds in deep complicity with his old confederate in the rhythm section, Bill Wyman, but the drummer's powerful swing is still a miracle of the millisecond deviations that separate a great rock drummer from a machine. And Keith's guitar, so superbly interwoven with Ronnie Wood's, remains the clanging, juddering, scything sound that will surely define The Rolling Stones' style down the ages.

Not that they do it all for love. Or not entirely. The Stones have been financial trailblazers as much as musical visionaries. Among the very first to explore the lucrative potential of tour sponsorship, of merchandising, webcasting and tie-ins with mobile phone operators, the band established a new reality in rock's premier division by earning a fortune from touring instead of writing the process off as mere promotion for the records. And just as they derived an ever-higher share of those ticket sales and CD royalties, so have their advisers secured some enviably low rates of taxation on the proceeds. (Don't forget that Jagger, the fitness instructor's son, is also an old boy of the London School of Economics.)

In fact, for a penetrating view of The Rolling Stones' role in the history of our times, I'd look to their financial advisor since 1970, the sage-like Prince Rupert Lowenstein. He regards the band as evangelizing agents of the momentous transformations that overtook Western society from the mid-1960s, 'where the prohibitions of the Decalogue were subordinated to the gospel of fulfilment of the individual's desires. The Rolling Stones' enormous popular success is a tribute to their ability to capture this taste and gratify its expectations.' In other words, when the Ten Commandments gave way to Aleister Crowley's dictum, 'Do what thou wilt shall be the whole of the law' – there was a Rolling Stones song on the jukebox.

One afternoon I'm taking tea in a hotel suite with Sir Michael Jagger, overlooking the Hyde Park lawns where the band played a legendary 1969 show two days after Brian's death. His eyes are twinkling deep inside the amazing crevices of his face. With great charm he fobs off questions about his wealth and his marriages, to talk lovingly of Chuck Berry, Slim Harpo and the blues. I ask about his sporadic solo ambitions, which once threatened to blow the Stones apart. 'You get to a certain point in your life where you just want to do things that you enjoy. Though The Rolling Stones is a great band, it's acquired a lot of baggage over the years…. It's a big committee. You think, I want to do this, like this, and I don't really give a hoot what someone else thinks.'

But The Rolling Stones will always re-assemble sooner or later. Mick and Keith co-exist like rival super-powers, knowing they have no alternative but to recognize and support the other. Charlie calls it 'a loving conflict': he could let it go, if he had to, and Ronnie would retire to his easel and paints. For Jagger and Richards, though, The Rolling Stones is the band they'll never walk out of alive.

Back in Chelsea, I ask Andrew what Brian was like. 'He was a pain in the arse. I'm sorry to tell you. Brian Jones was kind of like when they say a cat has nine lives, somebody made a mistake and sent him back for a tenth.' The reason their first leader fell by the wayside, and the others did not, is because rest of The Rolling Stones knew who rock'n'roll belonged to. It really is their property, and everyone else is only borrowing it.

THE ROLLING STONES 1962–1967

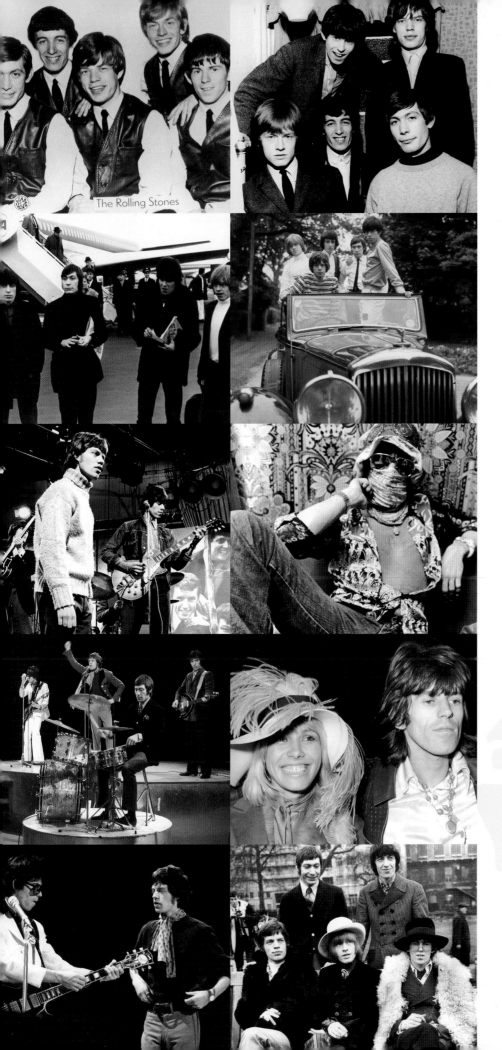

1962-67

Mick Jagger and Keith Richards had known each other since they were children – or, known of each other that is, having grown up in the same Dartford estate.

More romantically, Mick Jagger and Keith Richards met on a commuter train from Dartford to London in October 1960. An open love of blues and R&B was less common then as it is now, so when Keith, on the cusp of 18, saw his five-month senior carrying some Muddy Waters and Chuck Berry records on the train, he asked, 'You're into Chuck Berry?... That's a coincidence, I can play that s***.'

And so began a musical partnership that – against the odds – survives to this day. Checking out London's most enthusiastic blues scene over in west London's The Ealing Club, they would find Charlie Watts and Brian Jones sitting in with Alexis Korner's Blues Incorporated. This was where it was at – where whitey could sing the blues.

Within two years, The Rollin' Stones would have formed and played their first show in London's The Marquee Club, creating a London buzz soon after. By the end of the decade, and with the help of impresario Andrew 'Loog' Oldham, they'd become The Beatles' biggest musical competitors in a North vs. South, Safe vs. Dangerous, Clean vs. Dirty rivalry that saw the Stones posit themselves as riot-starting, establishment-baiting bad boys breaking every rule in Britain's book.

And that was just the beginning....

1962

July: FIRST GIG, LONDON

Dressed in coats and ties, The Rollin' Stones (as they were initially called, after a Muddy Waters song) performed their first live gig on 12 July at The Marquee Club, a tiny basement venue on London's Oxford Street. Playing an hour's worth of piano-driven R&B, they made £20 between them. The six-piece line-up included future members Mick, Brian and Keith. Ian 'Stu' Stewart – future long-term roadie and Stones session player – played piano, while Derek Taylor was on bass, and most likely future Kinks drummer Mick Avory played drums.

1963

January: CHARLIE WATTS

After declining offers to join the Stones for almost a year, Charlie Watts took Bobbie Korner's (Alexis' wife) advice and quit the band Blues By Six to play with the Stones at the Flamingo in Piccadilly on 14 January. Up until then, their drummers had alternated through players such as Mick Avory, Ginger Baker and Tony Chapman; but with the jazz-influenced Charlie taking over full-time, the Stones finally had a rigid backbone to support their R&B sound.

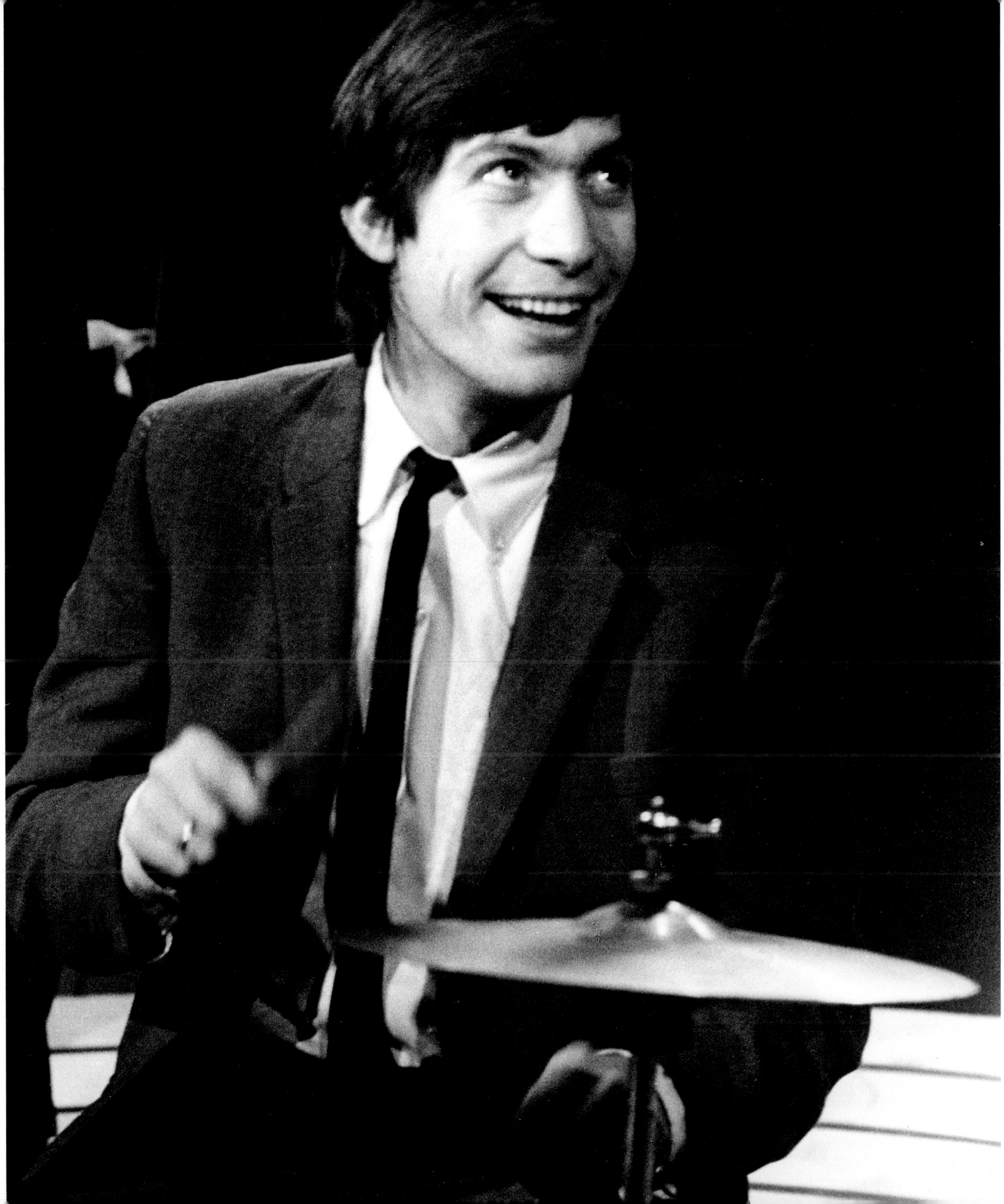

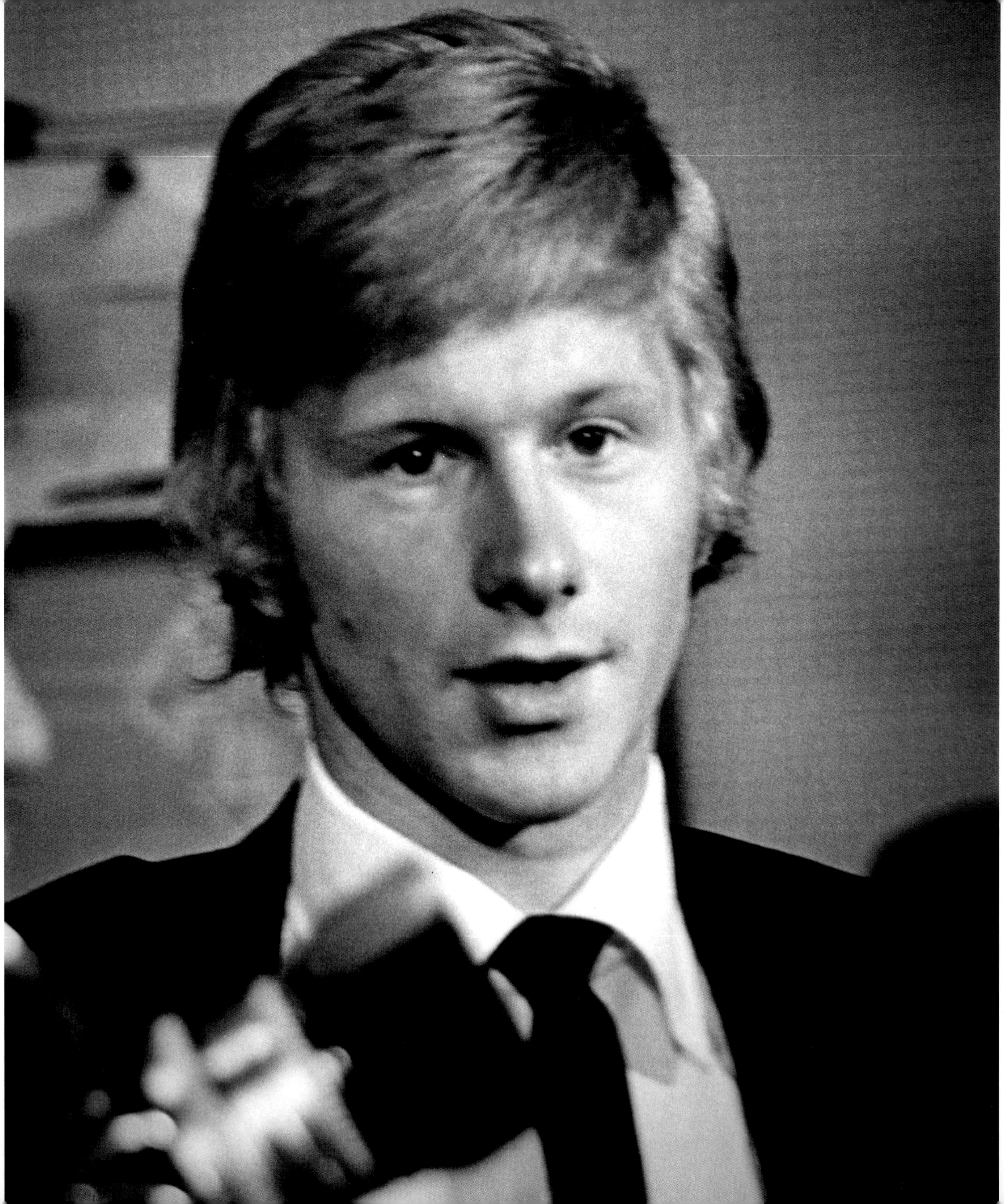

April: ANDREW OLDHAM

After seeing the Stones play the Crawdaddy in April, 19-year-old Andrew Oldham convinced them to let him be their manager, revolutionizing their look with an aggressive image that opposed The Beatles' clean-cut family look. Understanding that controversy sells, Oldham wrote the famous *Melody Maker* headline, 'Would You Let Your Sister Go With A Rolling Stone?', which gave the Stones the bad-boy image they would cultivate for the rest of their lives. Oldham also made them add the 'g' to make them The Rolling Stones, and wherever they went, he drummed up a controversy that made them sound dangerous and exciting.

May: SIGN WITH DECCA

Embarrassed by having passed up The Beatles, Decca Records were desperate to have a hot new band that could compete with them, and within a week of signing the Stones, Andrew Oldham got The Rolling Stones a recording contract with the label. By 10 May they were finally in the studio recording their first single.

The Rolling Stones

1964

June: FIRST SINGLE RELEASED

'Come On' – a Chuck Berry number that they had to re-record after
Decca were unhappy with the initial May recording – was released
as their first single, backed with Muddy Waters' 'I Want To Be Loved'.
Though it reached a respectable No. 21 in the charts, no one was
happy with it because it didn't capture the power of their live shows.
Mick later decided 'it was s***', and to Decca's annoyance the group
refused to play it live. Perhaps most importantly for this single, Oldham
had insisted that pianist Ian Stewart didn't suit the band's image and
so he would not be billed as a full-time member, though he would
continue to play piano and act as the group's roadie.

January: FIRST MAJOR TOUR

By the end of 1963 Mick and Keith had been introducing more soulful
influences to the group, and on 6 January they began their first UK tour
of major importance, supporting the Phil Spector-helmed girl group, The
Ronnettes, on the Group Scene '64 package tour. Spector himself
joined in February to monitor the girls, and was annoyed that Mick and
Keith fancied his lead Ronette and girlfriend (and future Mrs Spector),
Ronnie Bennett. Playing seven nights a week and travelling in a VW van
driven by Ian Stewart, the Stones' live show was so exciting that in
Glasgow they had to leave the stage three songs in, after a riot erupted
and trampled the police barricade.

January: THE ROLLING STONES EP

After a successful year which saw the Stones play live shows across the country, a large number of radio and TV spots, and a better-charting single with the Beatles-penned 'I Wanna Be Your Man' (No. 12), they released their first EP, *The Rolling Stones*, on 17 January. Consisting of covers reflecting their live shows at the time, 'Bye Bye Johnny' (set closer), 'Money', 'You Better Move On' (their first recorded soul cover, finding radio rotation on the BBC) and 'Poison Ivy', which reached No. 13 convinced Decca to let them record a full-length album.

February: 'NOT FADE AWAY'

Recording their third single in January, Keith had reworked Buddy Holly's 'Not Fade Away' into a Bo Diddley-inflected rave up. Already suffering from a punishing schedule, during the session the band degenerated into infighting, so Oldham called in Gene Pitney, who brought along some alcohol and a relaxed atmosphere, telling them it was his birthday. Though Decca didn't like the finished single, Oldham insisted it was a hit, and when it was released in February, it reached No. 3 in the UK, and was also their first charting US single, making No. 48.

March: 'AS TIME GOES BY'

Having seen Marianne Faithfull on TV, Andrew Oldham wanted the Stones to write a song for her. Reasoning that they couldn't rely on other people's songs all their lives, and knowing that they would have to compete with The Beatles' Lennon/McCartney songwriting team (the same team that gave the Stones their second single, 'I Wanna Be Your Man'), the legend runs that Oldham locked Mick and Keith in their kitchen, refusing to let them out until they had written a song. Keith later claimed that, desperate for the toilet, they quickly knocked out 'As Time Goes By', which later became a single for both Faithfull, and the Stones themselves.

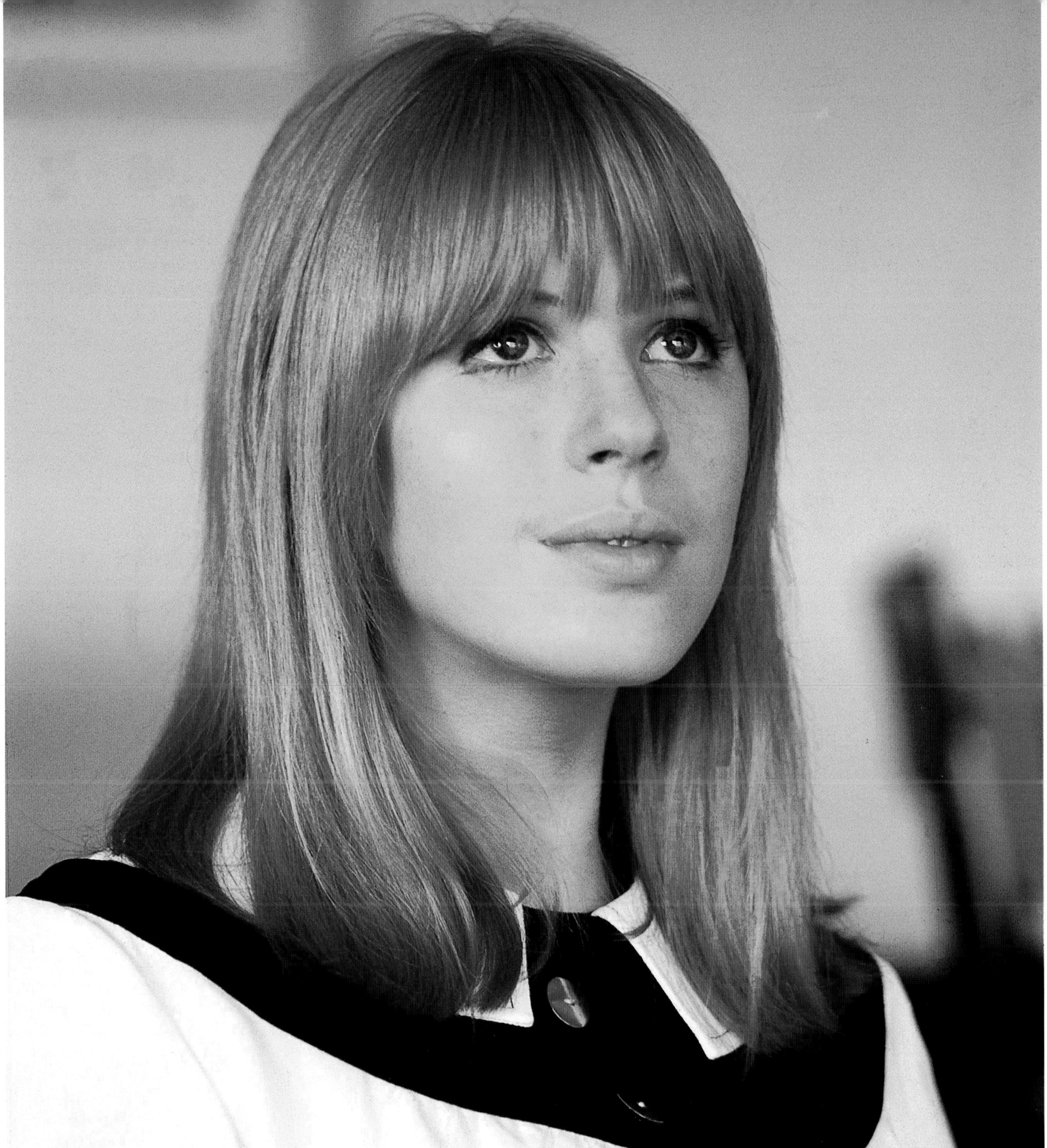

April: THE ROLLING STONES

'The Rolling Stones are more than just a group, they are a way of life,' read Oldham's liner notes to *The Rolling Stones*, the debut album released on 16 April (retitled *England's Newest Hitmakers* when it was released a month later, and with a different tracklisting in the US), and alongside the moody sleeve, it suggested the Stones' harder, riff-driven R&B; the antithesis of The Beatles' love-and-relationships output. Among the covers – which included 'I'm A King Bee', 'Route 66' and 'I Just Want To Make Love To You' – there was also 'Little By Little', co-credited to Nanker Phelge (a pseudonym for group compositions), and 'Tell Me', the first Jagger/Richards composition to be released. It knocked *With The Beatles*, their rivals' second album, down to No. 2 on the charts after its first week of release, suggesting that if The Beatles were the darlings of 1963, then the Stones would run amok 1964.

LIGHT PROGRAMME
ON THE AIR

June: FIRST US VISIT

On 1 June the Stones landed in New York for their first US tour. They were as well received in the States as they had been at home, and Oldham took advantage of passing through Chicago to book time in the celebrated Chess Studios. Legend has it that when the group arrived, Muddy Waters – their early idol and inspiration for their name – carried their instruments in, and was also whitewashing the building's ceiling for pay. Nevertheless, over two days they recorded enough material for an EP, some singles and much of their next LP.

June: 'IT'S ALL OVER NOW'

While visiting the States, New York DJ Murray The K (and self-proclaimed 'Fifth Beatle') suggested the Stones cover the Bobby Womack-penned 'It's All Over Now', recently released by his group The Valentinos. The Stones recorded it at their Chess sessions, adding a Brian Jones/Keith Richards dual-guitar attack, and gaining their first UK No. 1 with it by the end of the month.

August & September:
FIVE BY FIVE, 'TIME IS ON MY SIDE', 'LITTLE RED ROOSTER' AND 'HEART OF STONE'

Although still relying heavily on second-hand material, they were getting used to recording in the studio, with the *Five By Five* EP (five songs by five musicians) going to No. 1 almost immediately. It also contained two 'Nanker Phelge' compositions (one of which, '2010 South Michigan Avenue', was stripped of an impromptu Muddy Waters guitar part for contractual reasons), and the Stones saw out 1964 with a trio of singles, 'Time Is On My Side' (No. 6 US), 'Little Red Rooster' (No. 1 UK) and the second Jagger/Richards single, 'Heart Of Stone' (No. 19 US).

October: FIRST ED SULLIVAN SHOW APPEARANCE

The Stones' first nationwide TV appearance in the States took place on *The Ed Sullivan Show*, where they played 'Around & Around' and 'Time Is On My Side'. The group were not allowed to leave the studio building on the day of the performance, for fear that they might be mobbed by fans. Come transmission time, an estimated 70 million viewers watched the show. Parents were outraged by the Stones' bad-boy attitude and overt sexuality and wrote complaints to the show in their thousands: middle-America did not take to the band as they had to The Beatles' clean-cut image. The following morning, Ed Sullivan told the press, 'I promise you they will never be back on our show…. It took me seventeen years to build this show, and I'm not going to have it destroyed in a matter of weeks.' Six months later, the Stones played there again.

1965

January: THE ROLLING STONES NO. 2; AUSTRALIAN TOUR BEGINS

In the same month that they flew to Australia to meet a crowd of 3,000 rioting girls, *The Rolling Stones No. 2* was released in the UK (three months previously, *12x5* came out in the US, with a different tracklisting). With another brooding sleeve that made them look like they'd rather fight than hold your hand (the liner notes suggested mugging somebody for money to buy the album), it was another reflection of the hard R&B covers the Stones were playing live, with three originals and a soul influence with Solomon Burke's 'Everybody Needs Somebody To Love'. It stayed at No. 1 for 10 weeks in the UK.

February/March: 'THE LAST TIME'

'"The Last Time" was the first song we actually managed to write with a beat,' said Keith Richards of their ninth single; and being a perfect marriage of the Jones/Richards double-guitar attack, it made their third UK No. 1 (US No. 9) one of the most sophisticated Stones originals yet. Recorded in an all-night January session in LA, shortly before flying to Australia, it was also one of the first of many mid-1960s songs that Mick would write notoriously misogynistic lyrics for.

March: THE ROLLING STONES, NOW!

Containing many of the tracks from *The Rolling Stones No. 2* that *12x5* didn't feature (and some from their next UK album, *Out Of Our Heads*), *The Rolling Stones, Now!* was their third US LP. With more stark cover images, it reached No. 5 in the charts, and was a mix of UK singles, soul covers and Chess sessions tracks. More of a quick collection than an album proper, it helped keep US fans eager for their next fully original LP release.

March/April: EUROPEAN AND US TOURS

A two-week March package tour with The Hollies in Britain saw the violent female fan reaction step up a notch when one girl was launched over the balcony in Manchester, landing on more girls below and losing some teeth. The following month in the US, the fever continued as the Stones were truly spearheading a British invasion, with many shows needing extra dates to accommodate ticket demand.

May: '(I CAN'T GET NO) SATISFACTION'

'Satisfaction''s now-legendary fuzz-guitar riff was written by Richards when he woke up in the middle of the night with the idea in his head, and recorded it on a tape recorder for the morning. Soundtracking the older male's dissatisfaction in the mid-1960s, the single was initially hated by Mick and Keith (who thought it needed a horn section which, ironically, it received when Otis Redding covered it). It also troubled Brian, who panicked that the group was moving away from their R&B sound. But Decca loved it, and it made the Stones on both sides of the Atlantic, reaching No. 1 (though it was held off until August in the UK, for fear of competing with the *Got Live If You Want It!* EP).

June: EUROPEAN TOUR

The Stones set out on another European tour in June, covering four dates in Scotland and Denmark, and also playing in Norway, Sweden and Finland for the first time.

July: OUT OF OUR HEADS

Though it was their first LP to reach No. 1 in the US, the UK version of *Out Of Our Heads* – released in July – was a much more successful album artistically, as the US release was closer to being a compilation. The UK vinyl featured more exclusive tracks, and is also notable for being one of the last predominantly R&B covers-led albums that the group put out, as Jagger and Richards' own songwriting would become more prolific later in the year. Still, its importance was great in the US, where huge race riots were taking place, and it was less common for a white band to homage its R&B roots so openly.

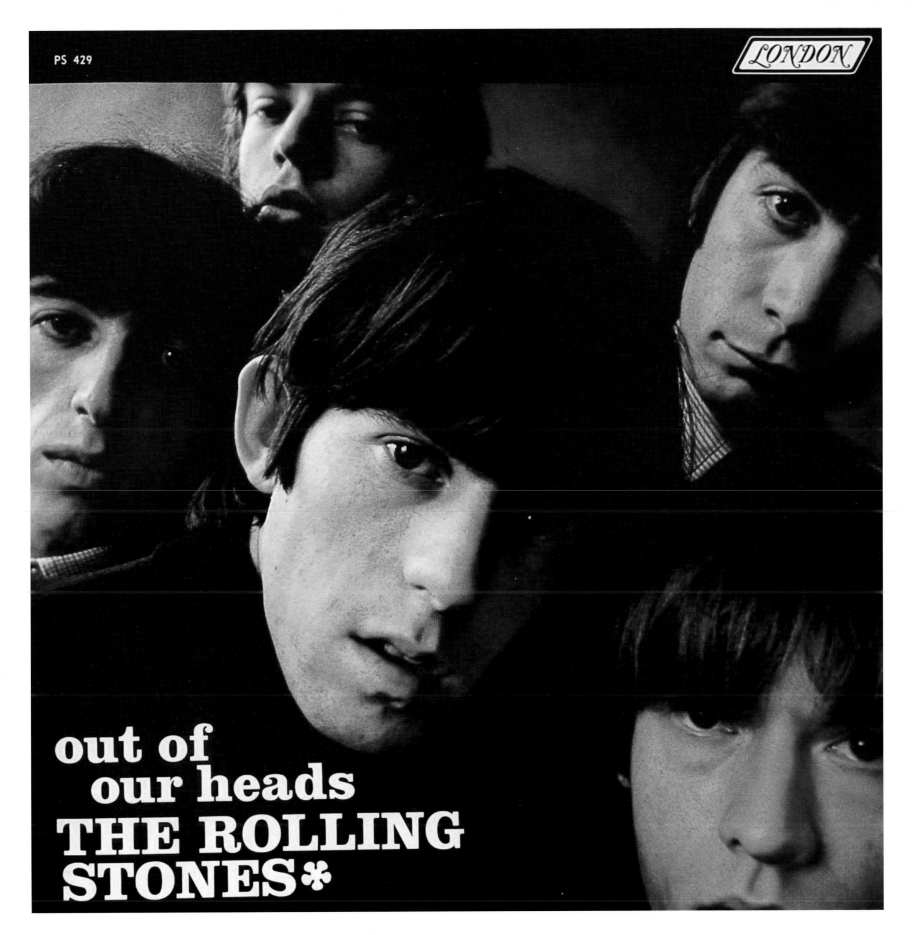

PS 429

LONDON

out of
our heads
THE ROLLING
STONES*

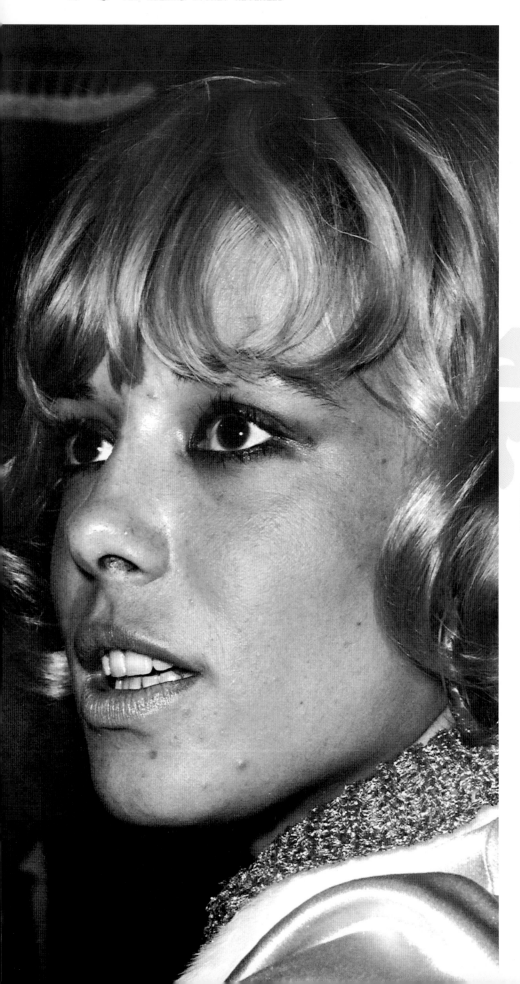

September: ANITA PALLENBERG

Brian – who was angry at his perceived growing lack of leadership in the band, and who had turned to drugs and alcohol in recent times to combat his insecurities – met Anita Pallenberg backstage at a September show in Munich. She would give him a much needed confidence boost for a while, as they became inseparable; and though Brian's problems would tear them apart in the end – seeing Anita turn to Keith in 1967 – their relationship was as intensely passionate as any of the Stones would have in their lives.

September/October: 'GET OFF OF MY CLOUD'

In Mick's words, a 'stop bugging me' song, 'Get Off Of My Cloud' was a more surreal, frenetic follow up to 'Satisfaction' that again reached No. 1 in both the US and the UK. Keith, again, didn't like it, feeling that it was rushed, but with a string of hit singles like these – and with more to follow – the Stones were asserting themselves, ignoring the much-celebrated political awareness of the era, and voicing the thoughts of a million youths who wondered what their country could do for them.

October: START OF AMERICAN TOUR

Playing fewer soul covers as Mick and Keith's own material started to rack up, the Stones took to their fourth US tour. By now, they were feared as a group of hard-faced, chain-smoking Brits who, unlike The Beatles, weren't happy to put up with journalists' mundane questions. 'Get Off Of My Cloud' was enjoying heavy radio rotation, and it helped them play places like Boston and New Haven for the first time.

November: DECEMBER'S CHILDREN (AND EVERYBODY'S)

Although the material was good, the US-only *December's Children (And Everybody's)* was more a compilation of new songs, cuts from *Out Of Our Heads* and old ones recorded as far back as 1963. Presenting the group framed austerely by large rubbish bins on the sleeve, it was actually one of their softer albums, including the orchestral 'As Tears Go By'. Brian Jones called it 'an album of rejects', and the group as a whole saw it as a disparate collection intended for the US tour, though only 'I'm Free' was still being performed live.

december's
children
(and everybody's)
THE
ROLLING
STONES*

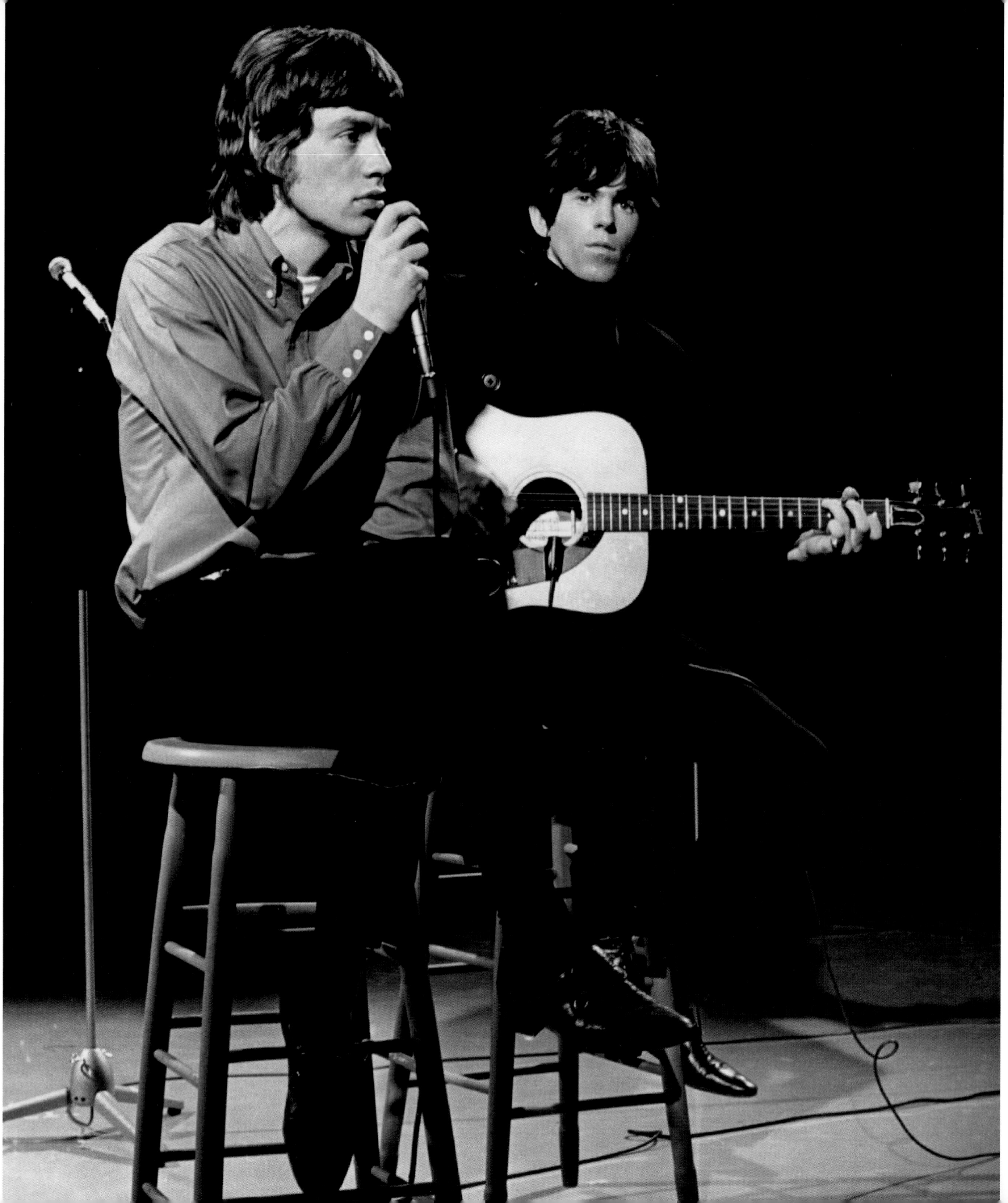

1966

January: 'AS TEARS GO BY'

The Stones' own version of 'As Tears Go By' – the song they wrote as 'As Time Goes By' when Andrew Oldham locked them in the kitchen back in 1964 – must have been a shock for an American audience that hadn't heard Marianne Faithfull's UK No. 4 release in 1964. Showing a completely different side of the band, it was a very early indicator of the ballad direction the Stones' singles would take in years to come.

February: '19TH NERVOUS BREAKDOWN'

The cynical worldview that the Stones were becoming known for in the mid-1960s continued on '19th Nervous Breakdown' (No. 2 UK and US), their third classic single in a row, and one that saw Jagger fix his acerbic lyrics on the type of middle-to-upper class lifestyle – and the kinds of people that live them – that he would target more often in the future.

February/March: AUSTRALIAN AND EUROPEAN TOURS

In February, a 25,000-strong crowd saw the Stones start a tour
in Sydney that would last until April, where it ended in Europe. The
fervour surrounding the Stones' shows hadn't abated, and on Brian's
24th birthday in New Zealand, the band were caught in a fan riot, with
Keith's face getting cut and Brian's leg injured when a group of girls
rushed the stage. Come the end of this leg, Bill Wyman would boast
that he'd slept with 13 girls, one of whom claimed that she'd had his
child the year before.

March: BIG HITS (HIGH TIDE AND GREEN GRASS)

The group's first official compilation, *Big Hits (High Tide And Green Grass)* came out in the US in March – eight months before the UK version, which would again feature a different tracklisting and sleeve.
Comprised of the Stones' biggest songs from 1964–65, it reached No. 3 in the US and remained in the charts there for two years.

March: AFTERMATH

A major artistic breakthrough for the group, *Aftermath* was the first Stones album to feature only Jagger/Richards compositions and was an early masterpiece, leading the group towards their unbeatable mid-period. By this point, the increasingly troubled Brian had largely given up playing the guitar, but he did contribute, adding extra instrumentation – like dulcimer, sitar and vibraphone – to his bandmates' songs, which helped make for one of the most textured and important albums of the Stones' early career. Although its lesser US release was cut from 14 songs to 12, it was pivotal in making Jagger/Richards compositions as important as Lennon/McCartney or Bob Dylan ones in the mid-1960s.

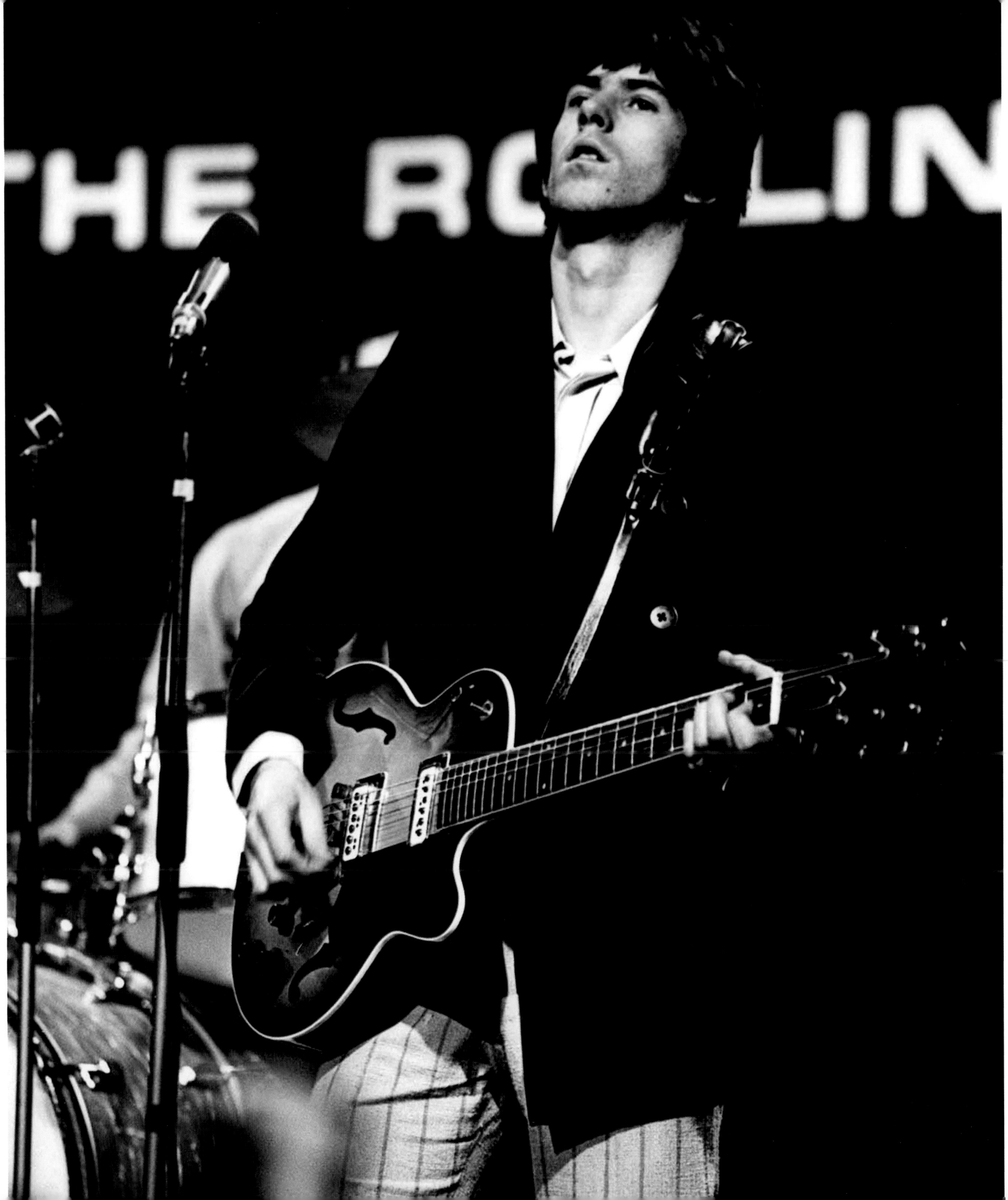
THE RO LIN

May: 'PAINT IT, BLACK'

Recorded during the pivotal *Aftermath* sessions, 'Paint It, Black' was an instant No. 1 on both sides of the water, though it was also their last for two years. The comma in the title attracted accusations of racism, but really it was a counterpoint to mid-1960s optimism, an existentialist's crisis and the greatest single the Stones had created up to this point.

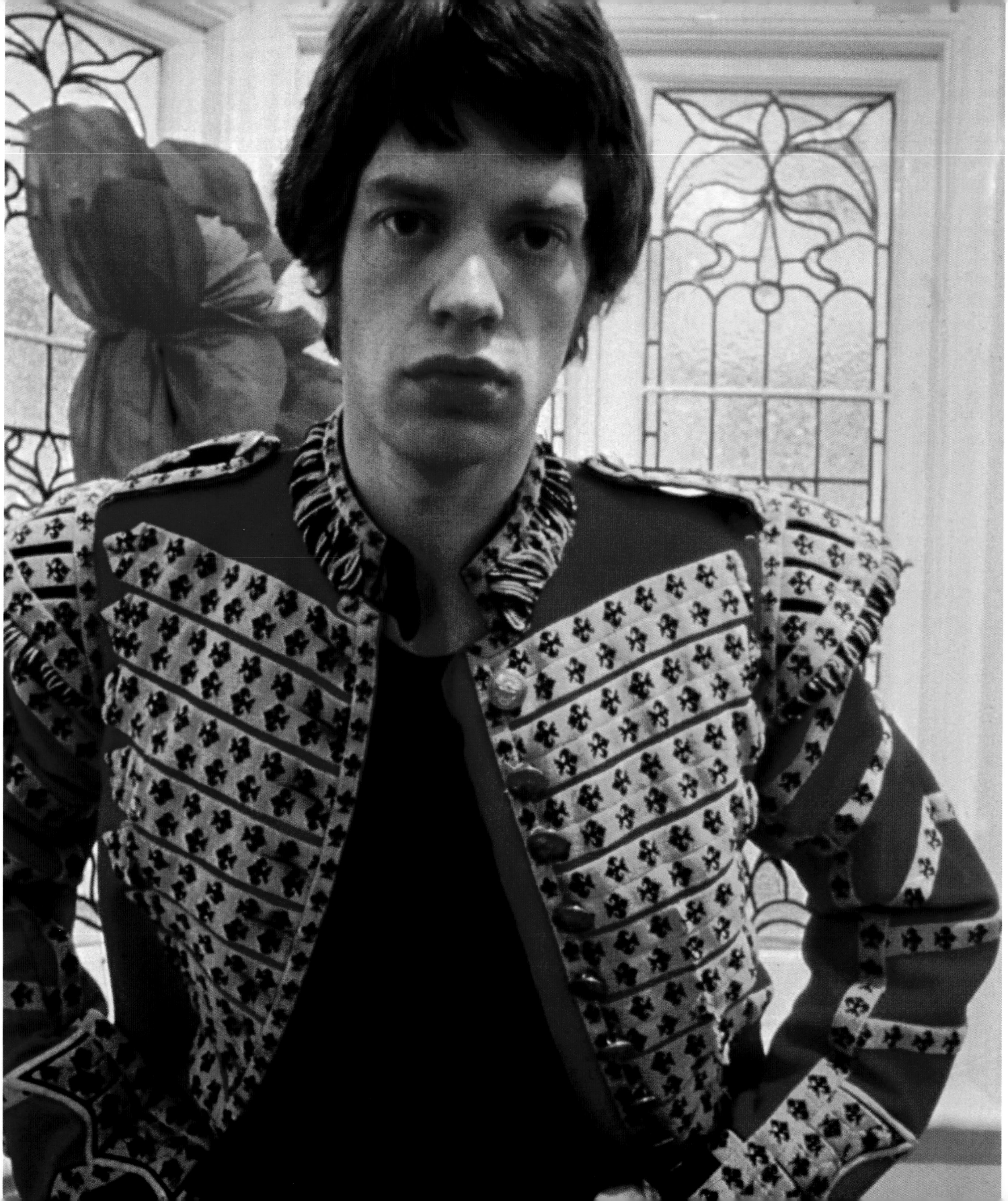

June: 'MOTHER'S LITTLE HELPER'

Echoing Pete Townshend's 'I hope I die before I get old' refrain, Jagger's nihilism deepened on the US-only No. 8 single, 'Mother's Little Helper'. It shocked many with its pointed depiction of middle-class housewives who escaped their humdrum lives by popping 'little yellow pill[s]', which were legal diet pills that also acted as a tranquilizer on those who took it.

September: 'HAVE YOU SEEN YOUR MOTHER, BABY, STANDING IN THE SHADOW?'

The Stones' social antagonism continued with their next single, with the group appearing dressed as Nazis in drag on the picture sleeve, and Jagger now even starting to focus on the most taboo of subjects for a pop song – incest. Nevertheless, its frantic, distorted, Hendrix-inspired riff (the group had met him a week prior to recording the song) helped it reach No. 5 in the UK and No. 9 in the US, while it ended their five-single attack upon social mores. The end of the month would see them begin their last tour for four years, where the rioting increased to the point where security guards would strike back at the female fans who tried to storm the stage.

October: MARIANNE FAITHFULL

Having been in the Stones' circle since Mick and Keith wrote 'As Tears Go By' for her at Andrew Oldham's behest, Marianne Faithfull and Mick had begun dating in secret, even though she was married to John Dunbar and initially fancied Keith. On 15 October, however, she and Mick made their relationship public when they attended the launch of London's underground newspaper, *International Times*. The couple would stay together until 1970 and be one of the more important and notorious of any individual Stones' relationships.

November: GOT LIVE IF YOU WANT IT

Despite *Got Live If You Want It!* [sic] being the group's third and final UK EP in June 1965, in the US, the exclamation mark-less *Got Live If You Want It* came out as their first live LP in November, despite the dubious nature of some of the recordings. Some were actually old studio tracks overdubbed with screaming fans, and although the sleeve stated that others came from shows at The Royal Albert Hall, it seems that they could have come from several shows at the end of their tour in October. The Stones subsequently disowned the album as being exploitative.

1967

January: BETWEEN THE BUTTONS

Much overlooked today, *Between The Buttons* saw the Stones start the new year with an album that had the ambition to match other period classics like The Beatles' *Revolver*, or Dylan's *Blonde On Blonde*. Building upon the eclecticism of Brian's additions to *Aftermath*, it is perhaps one of their most varied albums, though the group came to denounce it. Its variety of songs, however, make it appreciated by fans and critics alike, and it's also notable for being the final original Stones album to be released with differing UK and US tracklistings.

January: FIFTH ED SULLIVAN SHOW APPEARANCE

The Stones' first *Ed Sullivan Show* appearance in 1964 caused so much outrage that the host vowed they would never return. As with Elvis, however, Sullivan had to u-turn and invite them back more than once. Their fifth *Ed Sullivan Show* appearance would lead to arguments, when Andrew Oldham allowed 'Let's Spend The Night Together''s lyrics to be censored as 'Let's spend some time together'. In addition, the doormen failed to recognize them at the stage door (again; the same had happened on a previous visit) causing the group to be mobbed by fans. Mick ended up with his hand cut by a scissor-waving fan looking for his hair, and Keith punched the doorman.

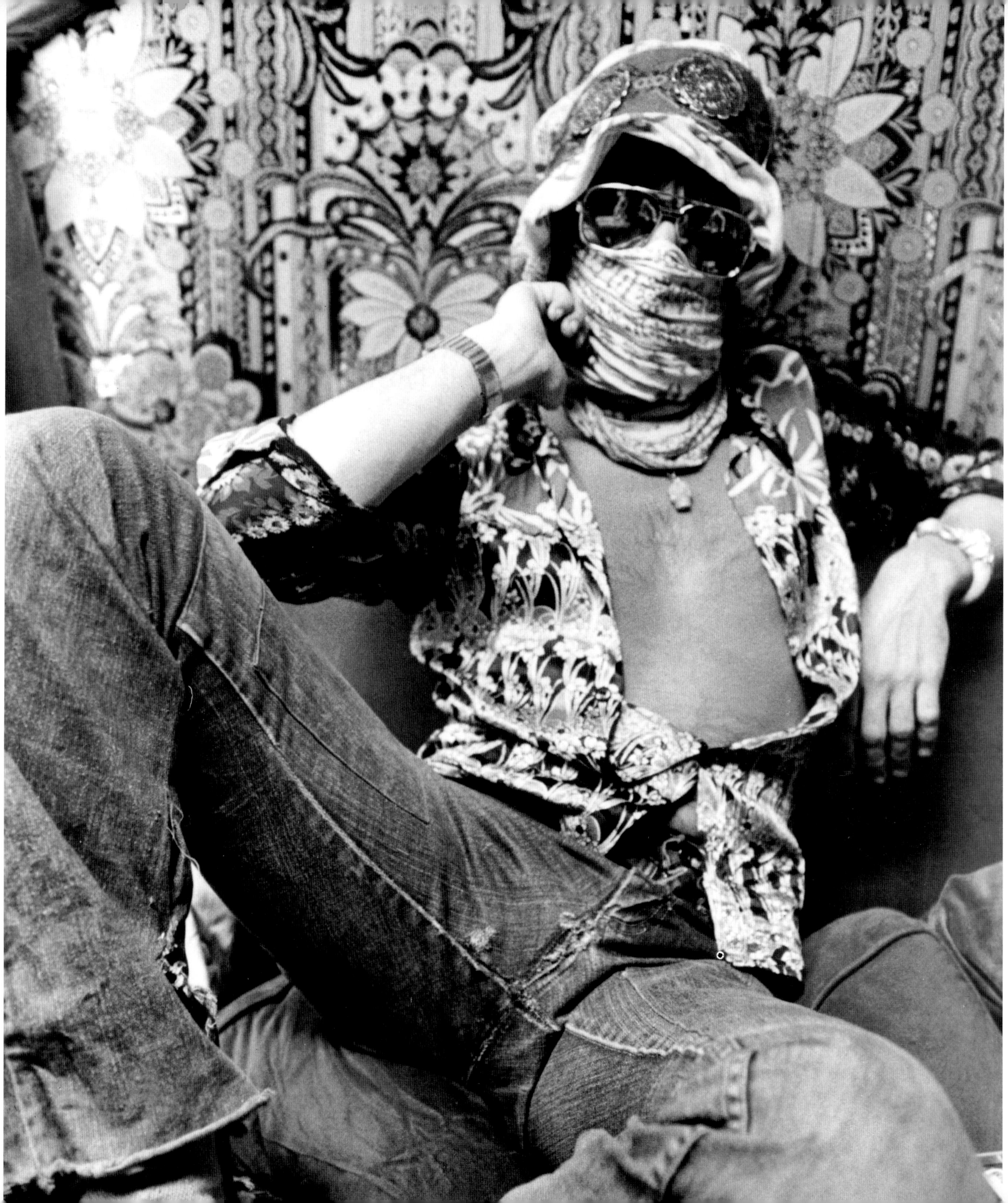

January: SUNDAY NIGHT AT THE LONDON PALLADIUM

Things were easier at home when, a week after their *Ed Sullivan Show* appearance, the Stones appeared on *Sunday Night At The London Palladium*. Keith and Brian allegedly played to the backing track of 'It's All Over Now' while tripping on acid, and the group refused to take part in the show's traditional goodbye wave upon a rotating stage. The show's producer claimed that it would insult both the host and the public, but they stood firm. Oldham tried to get them to comply, but he was only doing himself damage, as the Stones were getting increasingly fed up with what they perceived as him trying to get them to sell out and pander to the Establishment.

January: 'LET'S SPEND THE NIGHT TOGETHER'/'RUBY TUESDAY'

As was their custom, the single cuts were left off of the UK LP release, and their first double A-side, 'Let's Spend The Night Together'/'Ruby Tuesday' almost took them back to the top of the UK singles charts (they reached No. 2), but managed to top them in the US. While the former was a Mick-penned paean to oral sex that David Bowie would cover in 1973, 'Ruby Tuesday' was a ballad showcasing Keith's softer side, as he said goodbye to girlfriend Linda Keith, who had fallen into what he thought was a negative drug scene in New York.

February: REDLANDS' RAID

The police had been watching 'Swinging London' for a while, and were looking to combat rock stars they thought were drug abusers. Legend has it that only The Beatles were untouchable, and it is rumoured that they waited for George Harrison to leave before raiding Keith's Sussex home in the early morning hours of 12 February. Alerted by the *News Of The World*, who were out to get Mick after he motioned to sue them for claiming he used drugs (they'd mistaken him for Brian, who'd admitted to drug use), the police raided Richards' weekend party, arresting Mick and Keith for possession. It was after this that police officers spread the legendary (but false) claim that they had seen Mick eating a Mars Bar from Marianne Faithfull's vagina.

March: KEITH AND ANITA

An increasingly debilitated Brian Jones had put emotional strain on his relationship with Anita, while his mood swings caused the often-violent couple to get worse. Escaping from the police in Toulouse, Brian was hospitalized; and Keith and Anita checked into a room together, being driven to Spain the following morning, Brian's 25th birthday. It was the end of one relationship and the beginning of a dramatic 10-year one for Keith and Anita. 'A lot can go on in the backseat of a Bentley,' Keith would later say of the seemingly cold-hearted rejection of Brian. 'What can anyone say? S*** happens, man.'

May: BRIAN JONES ARRESTED

With Mick and Keith facing jail, Brian's paranoia convinced him he was next, losing a grip on his life, his position in the band he started, and his musical abilities. Ironically, the same day that Mick and Keith were formally charged with drug possession and for allowing a premises to be used for cannabis use respectively, Brian was arrested for possession of cannabis and cocaine at his London flat on Courtfield Road, singling him out as an easy target for future arrests.

June: JAGGER AND RICHARDS SENTENCED

On 27 June Mick was sent to prison, following a guilty charge for possession of speed; and the following day, Keith was also jailed, despite protests that the *News Of The World*, angry at Mick's lawsuit, had framed them. On 30 June, they were both bailed at £5,000 each by the High Court of Criminal Appeal. Robert Fraser, a friend who was also arrested in the bust, however, ended up spending four months in jail after his appeal was denied.

July: MICK ON TV

Immediately after receiving a probationary discharge regarding his drug bust, Mick was helicoptered to Essex to film a TV discussion for *World In Motion*. The other guests were William Rees-Mogg (author of *The Times*' 'Who Breaks A Butterfly On A Wheel?' feature that has been credited with saving the Stones from serious jail time), politician Lord Stow-Hill and John A.T. Robinson, the Bishop of Woolwich. The fact that someone as young as Jagger would appear on TV to talk about his situation in such an adult way helped raise the public's opinion of him, while also allowing him to remain an icon for 1960s youth.

July: FLOWERS

Another US album that amounted to little more than a compilation of singles or UK album tracks, *Flowers* came out on 3 July. Despite its 'flower power'-styled sleeve (with Brian's stem having no petals on it – a crude joke by Mick and Keith that highlighted his continuing alienation), the album was a more darkly themed collection of songs, hinting that the 1960s *zeitgeist* was not what it appeared to be.

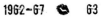

August: 'WE LOVE YOU'

Featuring John Lennon and Paul McCartney on vocal harmonies, and showcasing the Stones' new psychedelic leanings, 'We Love You' was released in the UK in August. A message of thanks to the band's fans who'd supported them throughout the drug busts, and a 'we don't care' defiance in the face of the police, meant it reached No. 8.

November: THEIR SATANIC MAJESTIES REQUEST

The first album release to be the same on both sides of the Atlantic, perhaps the most notable part of *Their Satanic Majesties Request* was the three-dimensional cover that it was initially released in. Although it takes in all the conventions of a 1967 psychedelic record, it was largely seen as an overblown and cynical attempt to cash in on The Beatles' *Sgt Pepper's Lonely Hearts Club Band*, and an ill-advised one at that. The fact that it was recorded piecemeal, under the strain of court cases and jail time, didn't help – something reflected in its inclusion of Bill Wyman's only original composition on a Rolling Stones release.

THE ROLLING STONES 1968–1972

ROLLING STONES LET IT BLEED DECCA

1968-72

After establishing themselves as mid-1960s contenders for The Beatles' crown, the Stones – unlike The Beatles – would enter the 1970s and embark upon their almighty middle period.

Being part of the Stones' circle at this point was akin to entering a vortex that led into a slightly inhuman world where anything could, and probably did, happen. Amid scenes of debauchery, Keith began a debilitating heroin addiction that would last the best part of a decade. Brian – founding member and blues purist, and who had begun his crippling addictions years back, thanks to paranoid and insecure character traits – would be dead by the end of the 1960s. Riots, death, tax exile and rumours of devil worshipping would surround the group, while 'The Rolling Stones' would begin to take on a life of its own – a power that no one could fully harness.

Yet amid it all, with Mick Taylor replacing Brian, they created the best music of their career. Penning enduring classics like 'Brown Sugar', 'Honky Tonk Women' and 'Sympathy For The Devil' would earn Keith the epithet, 'The Human Riff', and the run of four albums from *Beggars Banquet* to *Exile On Main St.* would be the creative peak that the Stones' legacy was built upon, and on which it still rests today.

1968

May: 'JUMPIN' JACK FLASH'

Built upon a nonsensical alliterative chorus – the conclusion of which is that everything's just 'a gas' – 'Jumpin' Jack Flash' heralded the Stones' masterful middle period, and took them back to the UK No. 1 spot for the first time in two years (it also went to No. 3 in the US). Demonic, voodooistic even, the song soundtracked the riots going on in Paris and was an all-attitude Tasmanian devil descending upon Britain and America, screaming *the Stones are back!* No finer single could they have recorded to stake a claim on their place as Britain's foremost rock band.

May: NME POLL WINNERS' SHOW

In May, the group performed a surprise encore at the *NME* Poll Winners' Show at Wembley Arena as a favour to their publicist, Les Perrin. Perrin had helped keep the police away from the band after convincing *The Times* to write a defensive piece about the Stones' recent police and drug problems. This feature ('Who Breaks A Butterfly On A Wheel?') has been praised for single-handedly saving Mick and Keith from further, and serious, jail time. At the *NME* show, they played just 'Jumpin' Jack Flash' and 'Satisfaction', but it raised the roof, and was to be Brian's last public live show with the band.

August: PERFORMANCE

Marking his first solo departure from the band –
something which would cause more trouble in the future
– Mick began filming alongside Anita Pallenberg for the
lead role in the film *Performance*, a psychodrama that
was deemed too offensive and sickening to release until
1970, though with hindsight it has been seen as a
classic British movie. Mick played a rock star bent on destroying the
sanity of a London gangster, played by actor James Fox. Adding to some
inter-band tensions was the fact that during a sex scene with Anita –
now Keith's full-time girlfriend – she and Mick actually performed the
act for the cameras, something which infuriated Richards.

August: 'STREET FIGHTING MAN'

 Perhaps it was just too violent, but reflecting the social upheaval and the clouds that darkened the flower-power generation as quickly as the sun had shone upon it, 'Street Fighting Man' was withdrawn as a UK single (it would be released two years later to reach No. 21), and it only reached No. 48 in the US charts. It called for street riots as a way to revolutionize society, and despite its chart performance it was another classic Jagger/Richards composition, and one that pinpointed exactly where 'Jack Flash' was heading.

December: BEGGARS BANQUET

Paring their sound down and taking in country influences courtesy of Gram Parsons, *Beggars Banquet* was a return to roots after *Their Satanic Majesties Request*, and featured Brian's last studio contributions of any substance. Its initial sleeve design – a toilet cubicle covered in graffiti – caused Decca to baulk, and demand that it be replaced with a white invitation-style design, which attracted more accusations of copying The Beatles, this time with their 'The White Album' on the shelves. With rock stalwarts 'Sympathy For The Devil' and 'Street Fighting Man', *Beggars* was the first in the Stones' unbeatable run of classic albums that lasted until the early 1970s. It was also the beginning of their descent into darker, druggier waters, and an excellent example of their being able to harness the chaos around them to good effect, and using it to reflect the state of the world, without being overtly political.

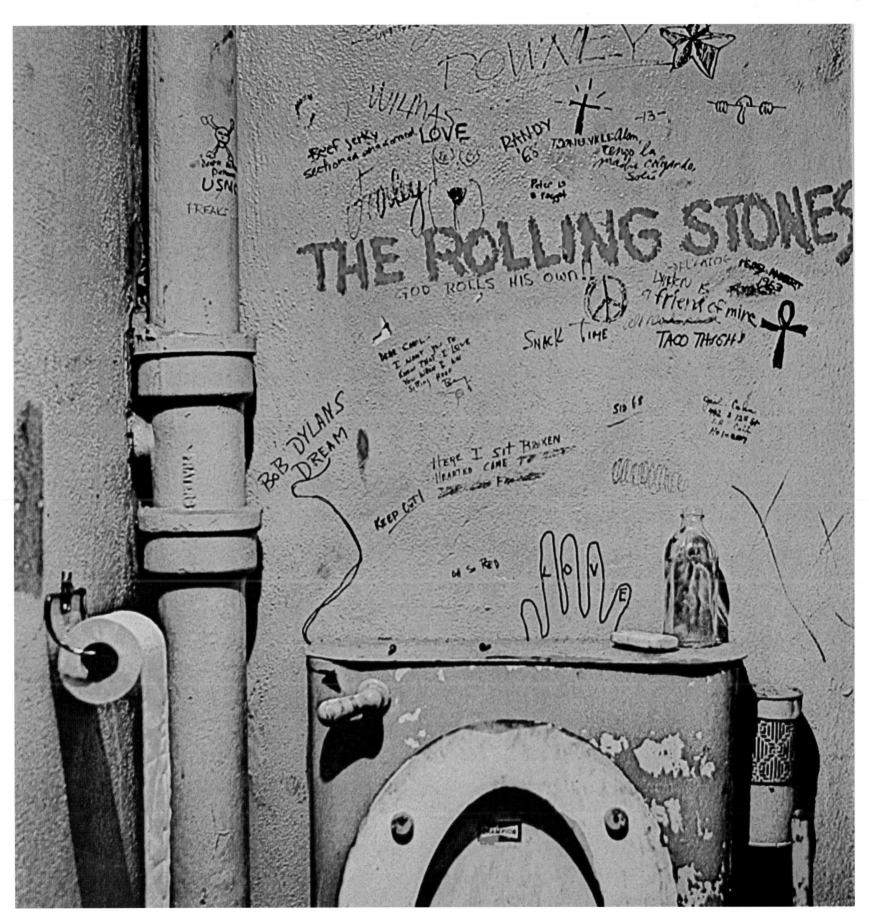

December: ROCK AND ROLL CIRCUS

Filmed over three days, 10–12 December, the ill-fated *Rock And Roll Circus* was meant to be an extravaganza, with the Stones headlining a show that saw the Lennon/Clapton/Richards supergroup The Dirty Mac, Marianne Faithfull and The Who performing between carnival acts. There in body but not spirit, Brian perhaps mirrored the burn-out the whole band felt at the time, and when watching the footage, it was clear that The Who had upstaged the Stones on their own turf. Allen Klein – an American businessman who had replaced Andrew Oldham as manager – refused to release the footage until its issue on VHS in 1996.

1969

June: BRIAN JONES AND MICK TAYLOR

On a hot summer's night, Mick, Keith and Charlie drove to Brian's recently purchased Cotchford Farm home and sacked him from the band. For years he'd been letting his paranoia, ego and drug addictions get the better of him, to the point where he barely played in the studio and wasn't stable enough to go on tour. With replacement Mick Taylor – a young, fluid, technically virtuosic guitarist – waiting in the wings to join immediately, the group softened the blow for Brian by allowing him to release any statement he liked, settling on it being Brian's decision to leave, as he was dissatisfied with the direction the Stones' music was taking.

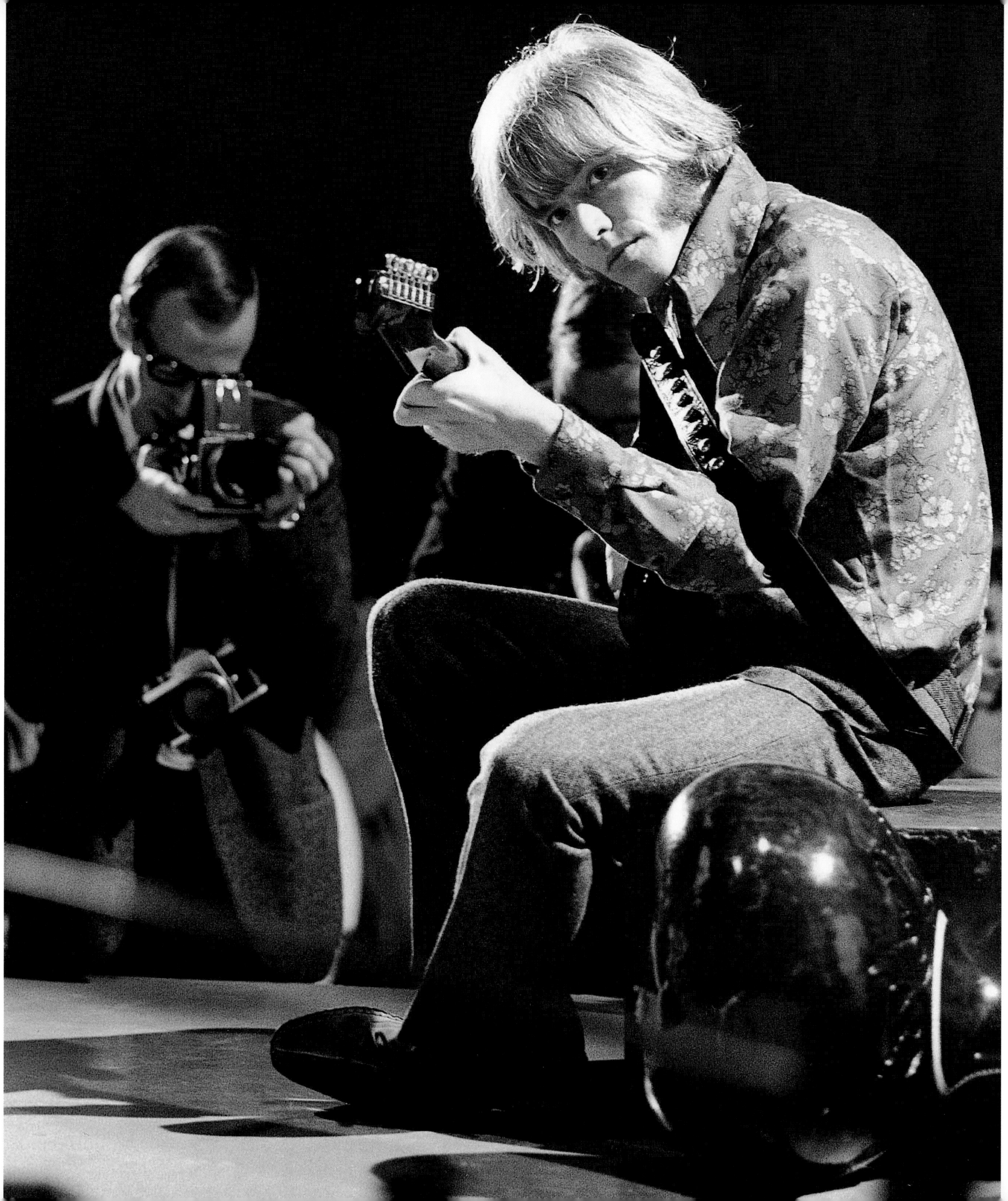

July: BRIAN JONES FOUND DEAD

There have been many attempts to untangle Brian Jones' controversial death at the age of 27 on 2 July. The official verdict was death by accidental drowning, but having proven himself a formidable swimmer on many occasions, something more suspicious surrounded the discovery of Brian's body in his swimming pool. Rumours that Brian was murdered have never been legally proven, but they continue to this day. Most commonly, people claim that Brian's builder, Frank Thorogood, then working on Cotchford Farm, may have drowned him.

July: HYDE PARK CONCERT

Three days after Brian was found dead, the Stones played their first full concert (initially to unveil the new band member; now in honour of the deceased founding member) in two years – a free concert at Hyde Park, to about 250,000 people. Somewhat ironically, it was shambolic. Mick, clad in a white skirted, party costume, read P. B. Shelley ('Peace! Peace! He is not dead...') to a restless crowd before releasing 2,000 white butterflies, many of which had already suffocated. They then preceded to stumble through an hour's worth of material before the group went their separate ways.

July: 'HONKY TONK WOMEN'

Recorded across five hours one night in May, 'Honky Tonk Women' dug deeper into the country influence that Gram Parsons and Ry Cooder were having on Keith Richards. Simply piano, horns, guitars and pedal steel, it was another No. 1 on both sides of the Atlantic, and has become the template for any balls-out, women-chasing rock'n'roll song since.

July: 'YOU CAN'T ALWAYS GET WHAT YOU WANT'

Recorded while Brian was still in the band (when he asked, 'What can I play?', Mick apparently replied 'I don't know. What *can* you play?'), a shortened version of 'You Can't Always Get What You Want' featured as 'Honky Tonk Women''s B-side. A plaintive reflection upon the druggy descent of the Stones and their entourage, it was given extra gravitas by the addition of The London Bach Choir as backing, and today remains one of the Stones' most poignant songs.

November: US TOUR BEGINS

 Their first US tour in three years saw the band's road manager, Sam Cutler, introduce the group as 'the greatest rock and roll band in the world'. Although by the end of the tour they were tearing out some of the best live music of their career, the beginning was fraught with sloppy playing, one night the amps blew and there were a number of on and off stage problems. Come the end, however, the Stones were firing on all cylinders as they prepared for a free concert intended to be the US equivalent of the July Hyde Park concert.

December: LET IT BLEED

Continuing with the country influences of *Beggars Banquet*, but turning the suspense levels up a couple of notches, *Let It Bleed* has frequently been lauded as the group's masterpiece, alongside *Exile On Main St.*: the revealing of the dark underbelly of the 1960s counter-culture, a Keith's-heroin-addiction-steeped album that encompassed the Stones' trademark cynicism, threats of violence and an energy that created, in Mick's words, an end-of-the-world record. Certainly sounding like a harbinger of the Apocalypse, the overall troubled ambience was no doubt helped by Brian's limited studio performance to begin with, and the subsequent piecemeal recordings the group attempted after his death.

December: ALTAMONT SPEEDWAY CONCERT

The hell of the Stones' free Altamont concert has never been forgotten. It dogged the Stones for years, and for some it signalled the death of the 1960s. Throughout the day a slew of bands played to a sweltering, thirsty crowd and Hell's Angels 'security guards'. By the time the Stones took to the stage, the Angels were drunk and lashing out mercilessly at anyone that got close. By the end of the night, four people were dead and plenty injured, but the worst memory would be the brutal murder of Meredith Hunter, a young black man who was stabbed once in the head and twice in the back before being stamped to death.

December: UK MINI-TOUR

Seeing the year out in between work on their forthcoming album – most notably on the songs 'Brown Sugar' and 'Dead Flowers' – the Stones would perform four London dates before Mick travelled to Rome to reconcile his relationship with Marianne Faithfull, though it would end again just as quickly.

1970

July: THE STONES LEAVE DECCA

After being with the label for years, the Stones declined to re-sign their contract with Decca, which expired in July 1970. At the same time, they officially announced that they would not be renewing their contract with the dubious business practices of manager Allen Klein, who they would later have to sue. Owing one more single to Decca, the group gave them 'Cocksucker Blues', which asked 'Where do I get my ass f***ed? Where do I get my cock sucked?' The label refused to release it, and Keith would later remark, 'I'd rather the Mafia than Decca'.

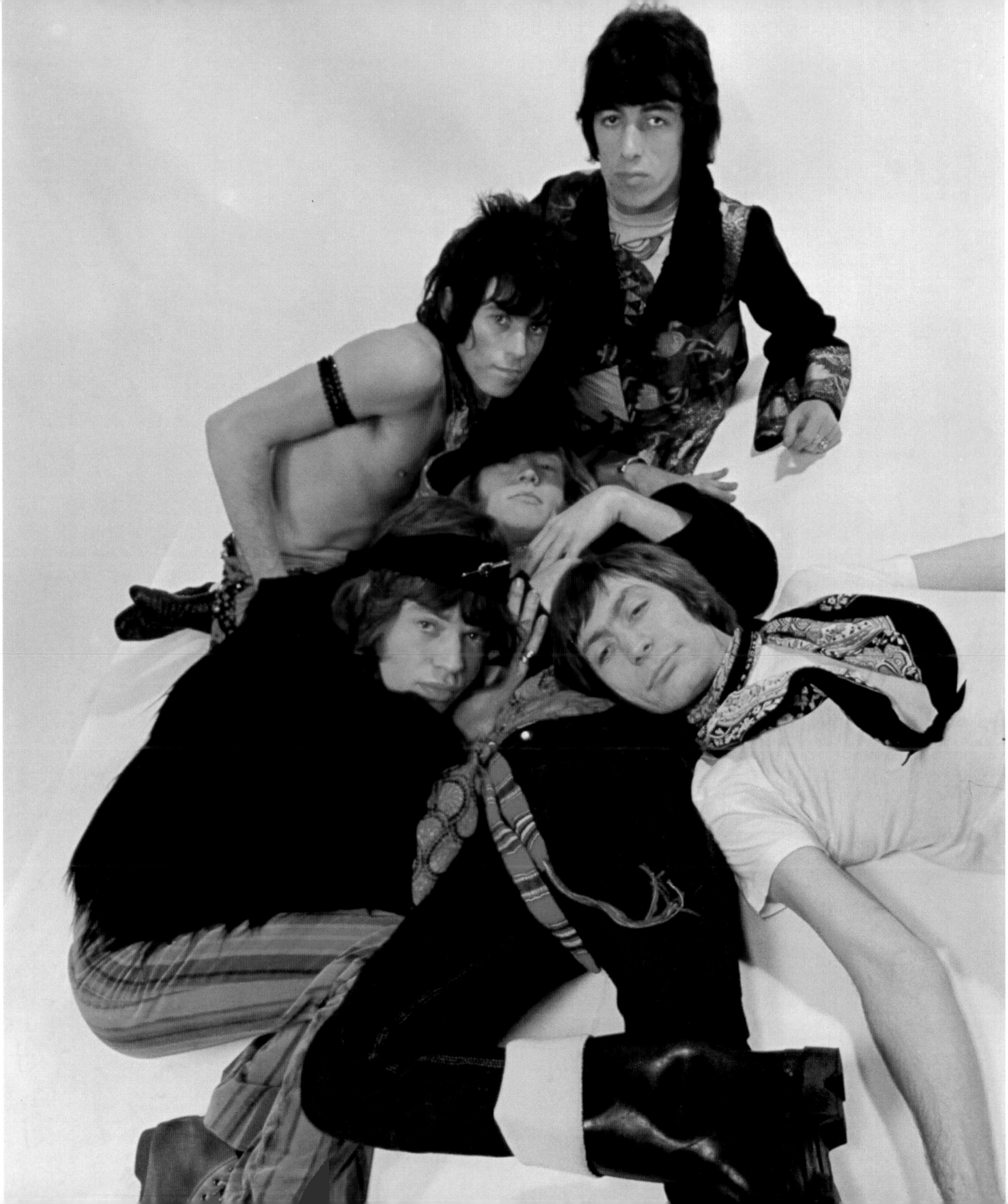

August: EUROPEAN TOUR STARTS

The Stones started their first European tour in three years on 30 August. Notably, it would see their first shift towards the large-scale productions they would stage in later years: high ticket prices, grand production values, huge entourages – both crew and hangers-on – and an augmentation of the Stones' sound with extra instrumentation, most notably saxophone players.

1971

September: GET YER YA-YA'S OUT!

While touring, Decca released *Get Yer Ya-Ya's Out!*, considered the group's first live album proper. Partly released to combat a bootleg recording, *LIVEr Than You'll Ever Be* – which even got a review in *Rolling Stone* magazine – *Ya-Ya's* was mostly recorded on the Stones' two Madison Square Garden shows in New York on their 1969 US tour, and it is notable for showcasing Mick Taylor and Keith Richards' live guitar interplay.

April: TAX EXILE IN FRANCE

Spiralling finances had been threatening to catch up with the group for years, and with band members owing a six-figure tax debt each, they were advised to become exiles. So, bit-by-bit, they moved their families to France. Keith set himself up in the Nellcote villa – allegedly stealing electricity from the nearby train tracks – near the Riviera, which would soon become a commune overrun by the band, friends and various shady characters, as it also became a home to Keith, Anita and their son Marlon; a drug den; and recording space for *Exile On Main St.*.

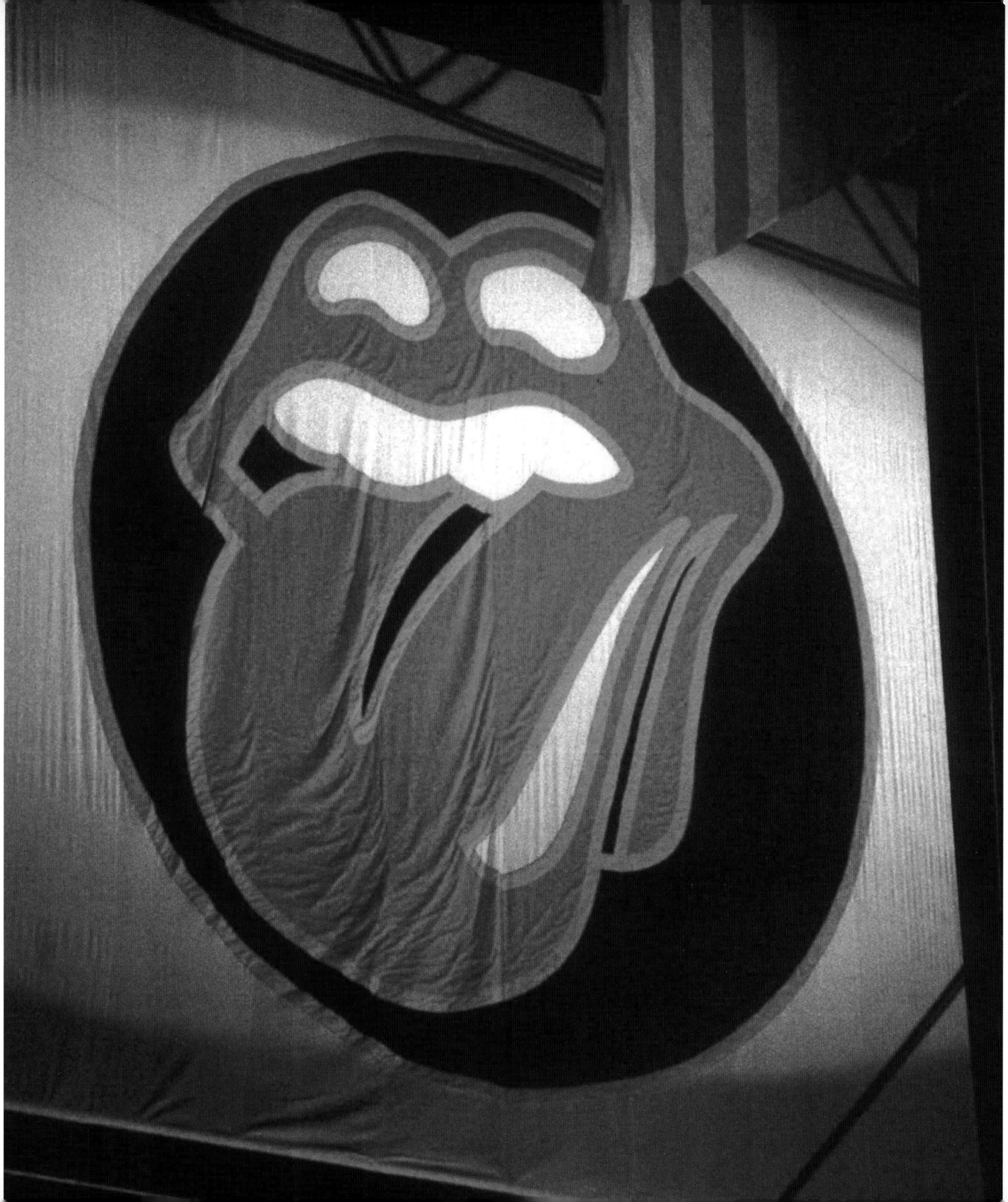

April: ROLLING STONES RECORDS

Sailing into Cannes to sign with Kinney National, an American corporation that presided over Warner Brothers, Elektra and Atlantic, the group formed Rolling Stones Records, for ever recognizable for its famous tongue-and-lips logo (not, as is often believed, designed by Andy Warhol, but by Mick Jagger and graphic designer John Pasche). Not a record label to sign artists in the way The Beatles' Apple was, Rolling Stones Records was just a way for the Stones to release their albums. Its importance lay in image as, coupled with the famous logo, it made them one of the first groups to be overtly aware of the market branding that would soon run the music business.

April: 'BROWN SUGAR'

Soon after signing their new record deal, the Stones released 'Brown Sugar'. Dating back to Mick's filming of the movie *Ned Kelly* in 1969, and debuted at Altamont, its title was a play on a type of potent Asian heroin, and the black girls that Mick found so attractive. One of the most compelling and recognizable songs in the Stones' canon, it reached No. 1 in the US and No. 2 in the UK, despite its slightly risky lyrics hinting at slave rape, heroin use and sadomasochism.

April: STICKY FINGERS

Hot on the heels of 'Brown Sugar', *Sticky Fingers* was released the following week. Showcasing a slightly made-over Stones (sax solos replace guitars; it was Mick Taylor's first full-length album), it was an instant smash – their first 1970s album, and one that would help the Stones stake a claim in rock camps on both sides of the Atlantic for the coming decade. (Incidentally, Rolling Stones Records' first release was actually *Brian Jones Presents The Pipes Of Pan At Jajouka*, seminal world music recordings of the Morrocan Jajouka musicians made by Brian in July 1968.)

May: BIANCA PEREZ MORENO DE MACIAS

Bianca Perez Moreno de Macias, Mick's girlfriend of nine months, was pregnant, and the couple married in St. Tropez, with Keith – who had tried to dissuade Mick from marrying her – as best man. For their time together, Bianca was disliked throughout the whole Stones camp, generally being seen as a haughty, spoilt bitch who looked down upon everyone else. Keith later claimed that Bianca was more negative for Mick than anyone realized, while Bianca would later state, 'My marriage ended on my wedding day.'

June: 'WILD HORSES'

Reaching No. 28, 'Wild Horses' was another ballad single popular with the US, and has since been covered by the Gram Parsons-led Flying Burrito Brothers, Guns N' Roses and Alicia Keys, among many others. Full of loss and written by Mick to try and win Marianne Faithfull back, it was one of his most open-hearted lyrics, and a signifier of Faithfull's importance to him – a marked contrast to Mick's cynical mid-1960s songs about the women in his life.

1972

April: 'TUMBLING DICE'

Inspired by Monte Carlo casinos near to Keith's Nellcote villa, 'Tumbling Dice' (No. 5 in the UK and No. 7 in the US) was a smoky jam telling the story of a gambler who can't remain faithful to women. As the public's first taste of the forthcoming *Exile On Main St.* album, it's interesting in that it saw Mick Taylor play bass in Bill Wyman's absence, and Jagger playing guitar. During the *Exile* sessions, Keith had often taken too much heroin to perform overdubs.

May: EXILE ON MAIN ST.

Completely schizophrenic, with slow blues, acoustic tracks and uptempo numbers, *Exile On Main St.* reflects its recording circumstances. Songs were put together sporadically and captured on the Stones' mobile studio, which they installed in the basement and used whenever Keith would record (his schedule was ruled by heroin and his son's waking hours). Still the best Stones album for many, *Exile On Main St.* was a sprawling 18-track double-LP that was also the fourth and final *bona fide* classic they would record, signalling the end of their great mid-period.

June: START OF NORTH AMERICAN (STP) TOUR

For their STP (Stones Touring Party; or Stop Tripping Please) tour the stadiums were getting bigger and the setup more elaborate, with a huge mirror erected over the stage to reflect light across the band. Keith, increasingly strung out on heroin, hated the tour and the large arenas it covered. Playing 90-minute sets of recent hits and *Exile* tracks, the group – all mostly wrecked throughout – burned out too easily, making it one of their more lackluster US jaunts.

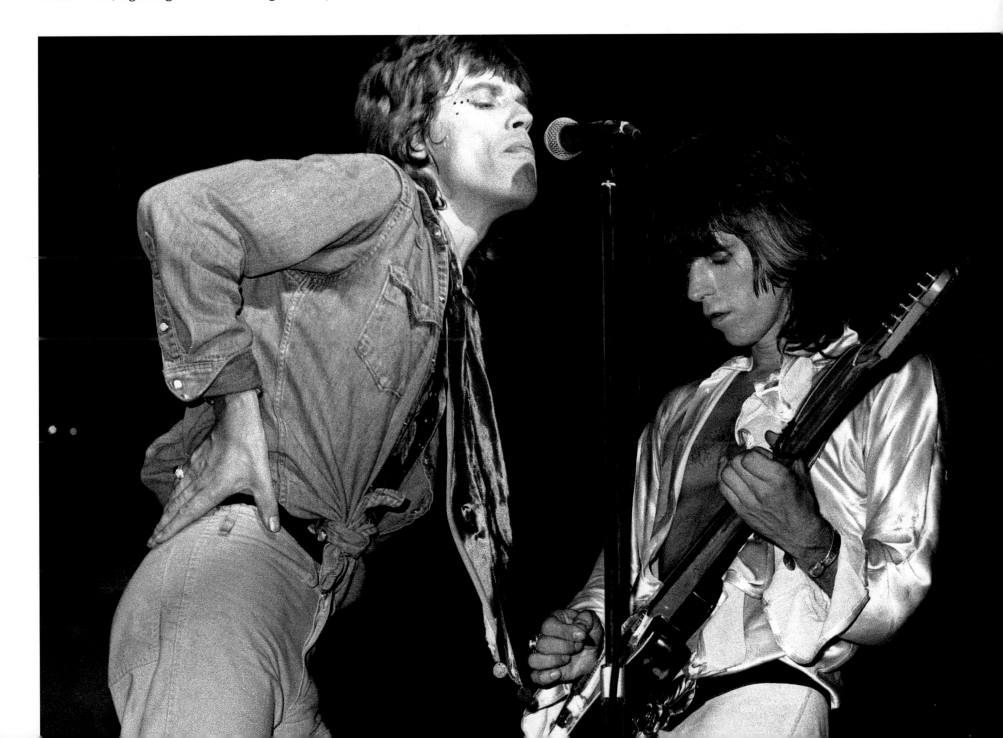

June: COCKSUCKER BLUES

Following the group around the US on the STP tour was director Robert Frank, who was filming a *cinema vérité* documentary that the Stones instantly vetoed upon watching it back, for fear that the sexually explicit footage, gratuitous drug-taking and other potentially illegal footage would cause them to be banned from the States. Though available illegally as a bootleg, rumour has it that there is a court order on the film that forbids it from being shown unless the director is physically present.

THE ROLLING STONES 1973-1981

1973–81

Despite having kicked off the 1970s with an early promise of continued success, come the middle of the decade – and into the 1980s – the Stones had to deal with greater problems, and their music would start to falter.

The musical ground was shifting, as hard-rock stadium acts like Led Zeppelin revolutionized the concept of touring, forcing the Stones to keep up with the new breed. Keith's drug addiction became all-encompassing, resulting in an infamous 1977 arrest in Toronto, so Jagger took band leadership duties upon himself, turning the Stones into a somewhat radio-friendly ballads group for the States. Replacing the skill of writing classic songs with a live spectacle, they would become a near-parody of themselves through 1970s stadium tours, and were often unable to live up to the 'greatest rock and roll band in the world' tag they once filled so well.

Mick Taylor would leave, Ron Wood would join, and the Stones' existence became more like that of a rolling circus troupe looking for good times, than a vital rock band for the 1970s. With a major creative resurgence in 1978's *Some Girls* album, they tapped into the burgeoning disco market. But it would take more than one album to keep them going strong, and by 1981's *Tattoo You*, Mick and Keith would have to rely, for the first time, on years-old material for a new album.

1973

January/February:
NICARAGUA, HAWAII, NEW ZEALAND AND AUSTRALIA

Plans to tour the Far East were hampered when Tokyo refused to let convicted drug users Mick and Keith into the country. Performing an Earthquake Relief Benefit concert in Nicaragua as a warm-up show, the group then played two shows in Hawaii. They filled the Tokyo gap by travelling to LA to work on new songs, before playing Hong Kong, Australia (who decided to lift a ban similar to Tokyo's) and New Zealand.

May: MEET RON WOOD

Out at London's Tramps club one night, Keith bumped into Chrissie Wood, the beautiful blonde wife of Ronnie Wood – guitarist in The Faces, the Rod Stewart-fronted pub-rock band that had risen from the ashes of The Small Faces. Inviting Richards inside after he gave her a lift home, his initial thoughts of having a good time with Wood's wife were quashed when, being led into the house's basement studio, he met up with Ron himself, who, significantly, was working with Mick Jagger on the song that would become 'It's Only Rock'n'Roll'.

August: GOATS HEAD SOUP

With many *Goats Head Soup* tracks being born in Jamaica, where Mick and Keith had spent a lot of time since *Exile*, it was no surprise that the album – one which began the Stones' 'lean period' – saw them focus less on their songwriting, and more on establishing grooves. Ian Stewart called it 'bloody insipid' upon release, though it included a few worthy tracks; and while songs like 'Starfucker' (retitled 'Star Star' on the sleeve) caused some controversy, it certainly lacked the flame of their previous four albums.

August: 'ANGIE'

Mistakenly believed to be written for David Bowie's wife Angie, the song was actually written for Anita Pallenberg, and was the Stones' first US No. 1 in five years (since 'Honky Tonk Women'). Awash with strings, it became the Stones' biggest radio-friendly ballad to date, reaching No. 5 in the UK. With Keith's heroin use beginning to consume him, 'Angie' was noteworthy for being the moment of Jagger's most overt taking control of the band – something that would continue well into the 1980s – and the moment where, on radio at least, the Stones became a softer ballads band.

September: GOATS HEAD SOUP TOUR STARTS

Perhaps their most depraved tour so far (even Mick Taylor had begun using heroin), the Stones set out across Europe through September to October. Keith was entering one of his lowest points, arguing with Anita, and forgetting the words to 'Happy' – his song from *Exile* – on most nights. In Switzerland, he and Marshall Chess – head of Rolling Stones Records and son of Chess label founder Leonard – went on a three-day treatment that filtered heroin from their bloodstreams, which led to rumours that Keith was receiving blood transfusions to allow his continued heroin intake. Rumours also spread that he was going to be the next major rock'n'roll death, following Jimi Hendrix, Janis Joplin, Jim Morrison and, of course, Brian Jones.

October: BRUSSELS RECORDINGS

Throughout October the group made some recordings for a proposed live album, and on 19 October, they played Berlin's Deutschlandhalle, which turned out to be Mick Taylor's last live show with the band. Bill Wyman had also let it be known that this could be his last tour.

1974

July: 'IT'S ONLY ROCK'N'ROLL' (SINGLE)

With input from Ronnie Wood – who, true to the Stones' dubious crediting practices, was listed as having merely 'inspired' the song – 'It's Only Rock'n'Roll' was a joyous piece of fluff in comparison to their earlier work; and though it had a catchy hook ('It's only rock'n'roll but I like it…'), it only reached No. 10 in the UK (and No. 16 in the US), their lowest UK chart placing since their first single, 'Come On', which had reached No. 21 11 years previously.

October: IT'S ONLY ROCK'N'ROLL (ALBUM)

Failing to energize the band fully and lift them from their fallow period, the *It's Only Rock'n'Roll* album – the first of many with production credited to 'The Glimmer Twins', a pseudonym for Mick and Keith and their jet-set, rock-star partnership – would be Mick Taylor's last, and was largely a collection of riffs looking for songs, some Jamaican ska influence and a mess of unfocused ideas. Mick, virtually in charge of the band now, refused to let them go out on tour, which annoyed Keith, though he was in no condition to do or plan anything of note.

November: MICK TAYLOR QUITS

After storming out of a fruitless band meeting in October, Mick Taylor left the group, partly out of boredom (they hadn't toured in a year), a desire to record his own albums, and disappointment. He'd never really fitted in, and recording had become more painful than enjoyable (by way of persecution, Keith would often wipe guitar lines Taylor had laid down during the *It's Only Rock'n'Roll* sessions). Handing in his notice as plans were being made for a 1975 tour, and just before starting new studio work, which infuriated Keith, who declared, 'No one leaves this band except in a f***ing pine box.'

1975

March: RON WOOD JOINS

Having been friendly with the Stones since May 1973, Ron Wood agreed to join the group – initially temporarily – to help out on their forthcoming American tour, though he might as well have been hired as a full-time member straightaway. While not the soloist that Mick Taylor was, he had the perfect temperament to smooth over any band disagreements, and got on with Keith like a house on fire. At once younger brother, jester and partyman, 'Woody' had the perfect personality to join the group that seemed to be cracking slightly at the seams.

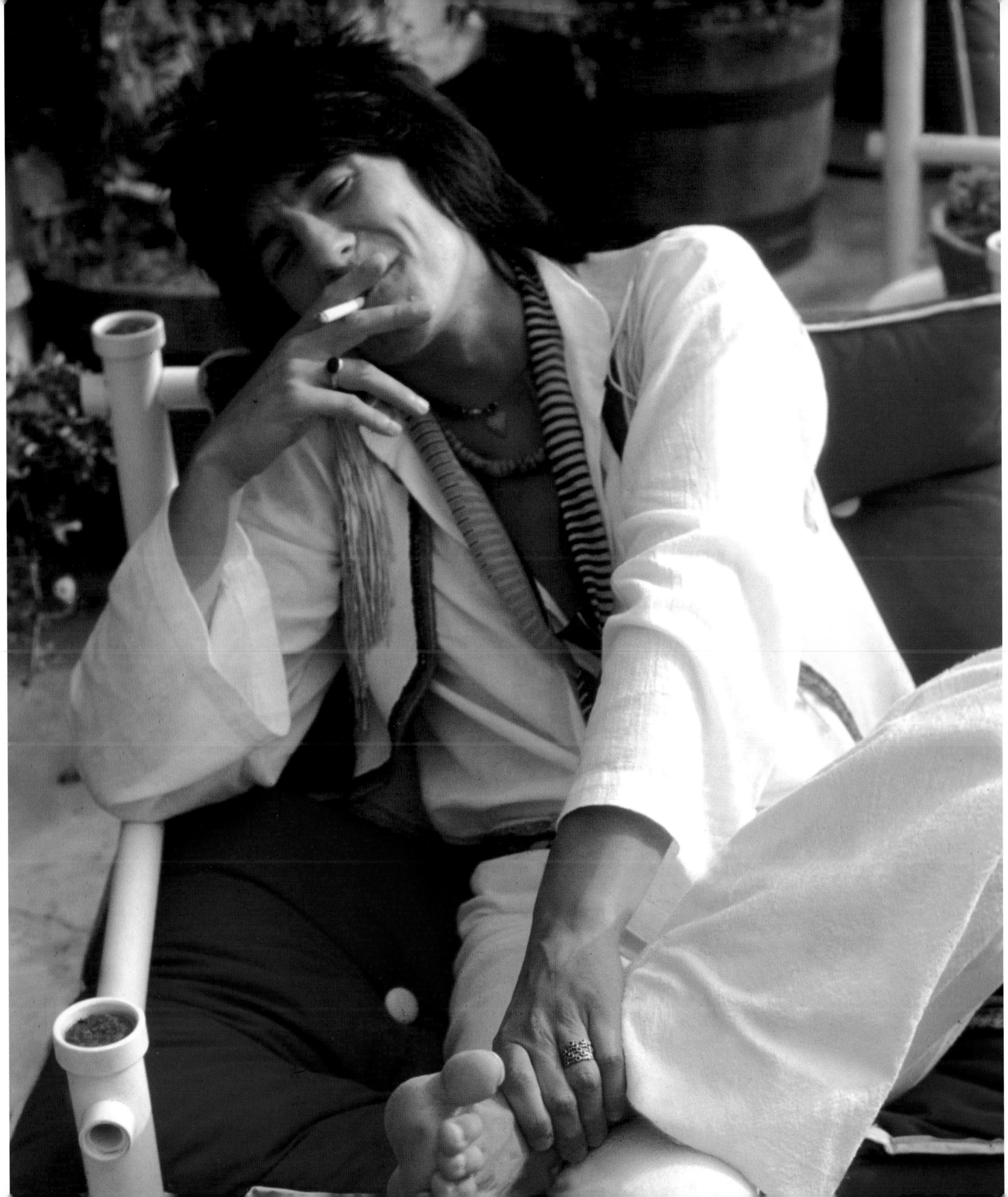

June: TOTA

The funk-tinged TOTA – Tour Of The Americas, initially scheduled to cover South American countries as well as North America – was a rolling cavalcade of stoned and drunk party animals resting on their laurels and playing 47 dates across 27 venues with a 'loose-lips-cost-wives' policy, and an overriding ambition to make money. Using props for the first time, and to self-parodying proportions, there were 'Who the f*** is Mick Jagger?' T-shirts; a stage designed as a lotus plant that opened up with the band inside; Mick riding a massive blow-up penis to 'Starfucker' and sometimes swinging out above the crowd, Tarzan-style; and even a row of elephants acting as security one night. Job done, the group dispersed for most of the remaining year.

June: METAMORPHOSIS

Compiled without the band's involvement – and by Allen Klein, who took over control of their Decca recordings in 1970 – *Metamorphosis* was a collection of outtakes, alternate recordings of well-known Stones songs and largely a cash-in on the Stones' US tour. It managed to make No. 12 in the States, but limped to No. 45 in the UK.

1976

April: 'FOOL TO CRY'

Another Jagger ballad as an album's first single, 'Fool To Cry' was Mick's lamenting for a woman he loved, from an impoverished part of the city he lived, but was convincing enough for it to go Top 10 worldwide and introduce the simultaneously released *Black And Blue* album.

April: BLACK AND BLUE

By now having to compete with the rock juggernaut of Led Zeppelin and their hard-rock offspring, *Black And Blue* was a funk and reggae-influenced album, showcasing Mick's interest in both the former and the popular disco market, and Keith's immersion in the latter. Largely a collection of jam-based songs, legendary rock critic Lester Bangs would damn it as being the 'first meaningless Stones album', writing, 'they are perfectly in tune with the times … the heat's off … they really don't matter anymore'.

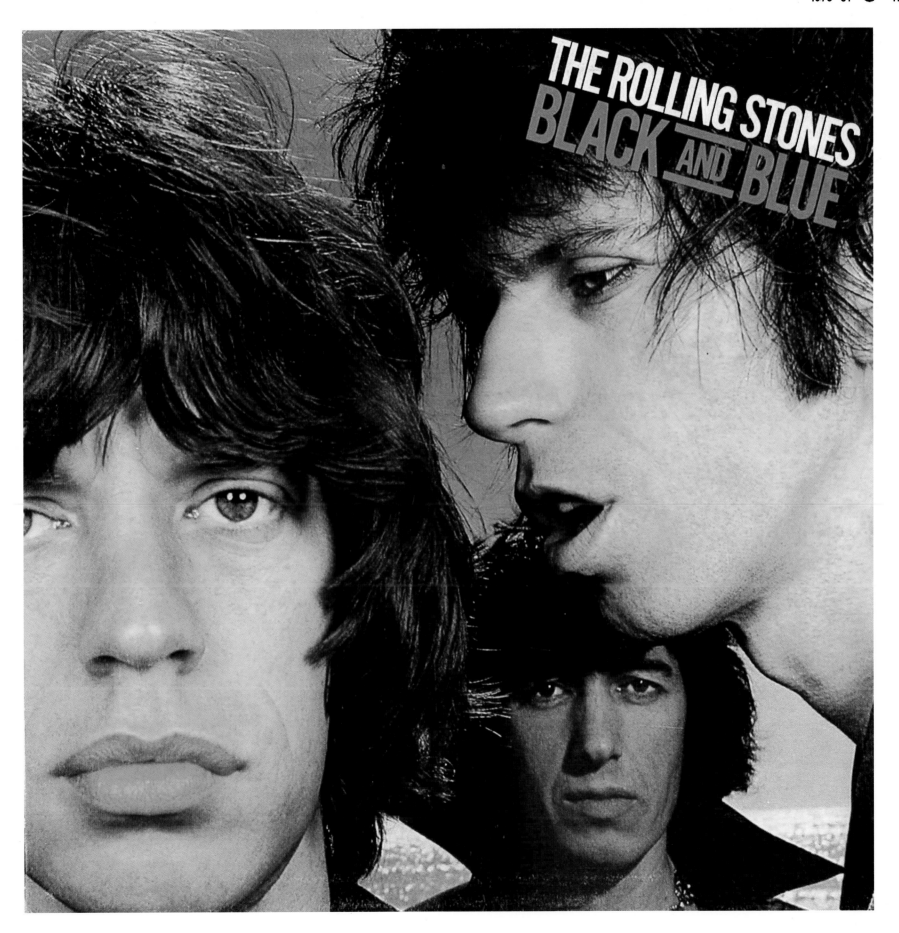

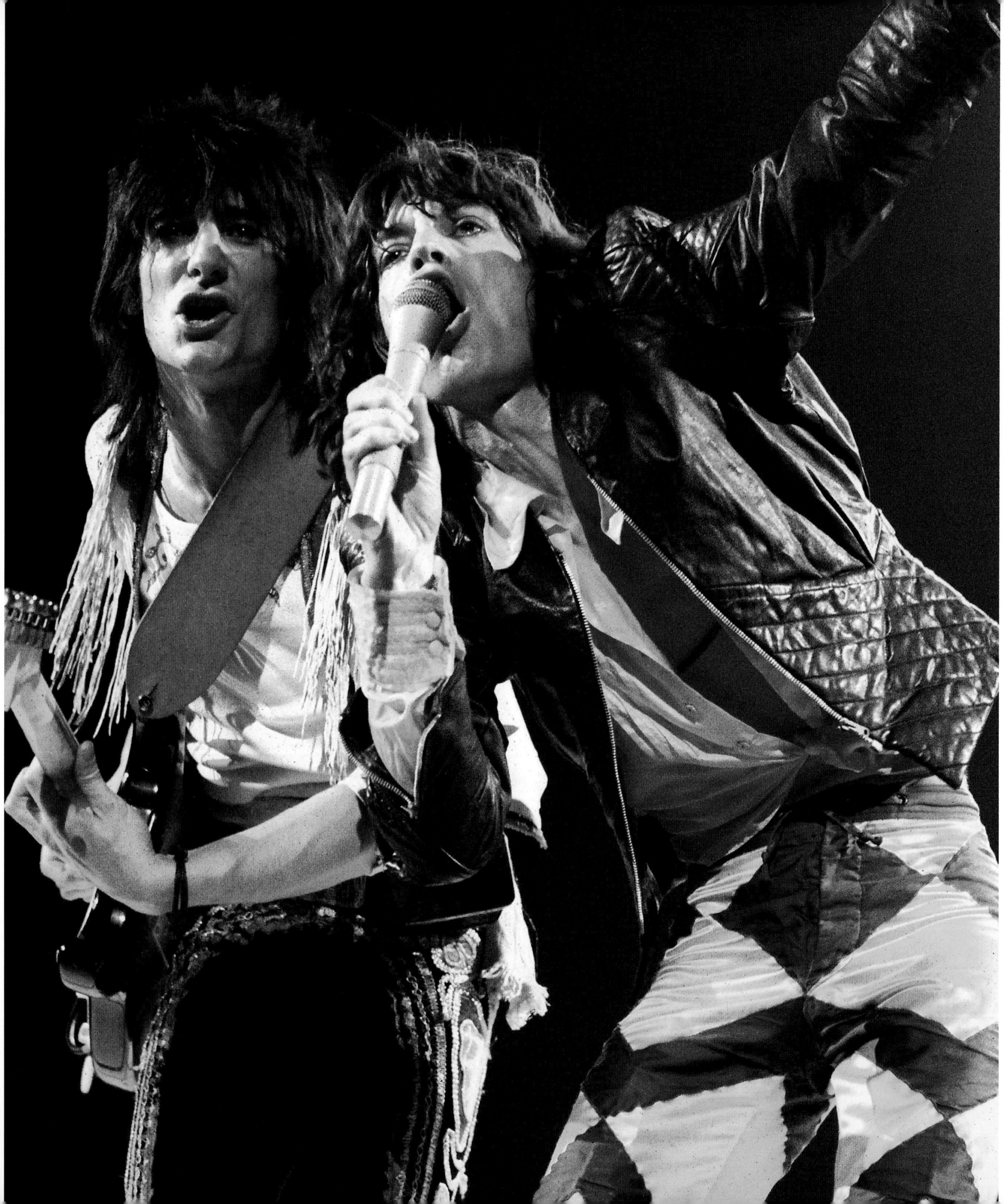

April: START OF EUROPEAN TOUR

An eight-week European tour saw the Stones' crew multiply to 100 (most of whom were also on heroin throughout), with Keith strung out and frequently awake for days on end – even falling asleep during some shows. No one can be said to have played much great music, as the group were at one of their most decadent points, mostly going through the motions of touring. Devastatingly, however, at their final Paris show in June, Keith was informed that his son Tara, then just 11 weeks old, had suffocated in his sleep, which prompted one of his best performances of the tour.

1977

February: KEITH ARRESTED IN TORONTO

With a strong live album emerging from the haphazard European tour, Mick had decided the band should meet in Toronto to record a few small club dates for the live release. With Keith and Anita's relationship resembling a living hell, they holed up in the group's Toronto hotel. Acting on a tip, the Royal Canadian Mounted Police descended upon Keith, who had passed out in one of the rooms, resuscitating him long enough to arrest him for having sufficient heroin to be charged as a drug dealer.

    Amazingly, not only did America let him into the country to join a rehab clinic almost immediately, but when the case came to trial in October 1978, Keith was practically let off. His stated legend is that a blind girl, Rita – who had followed the Stones to every show on the 1975 TOTA, and whom Keith had taken great care of each night – was related to the judge, and told him what Keith had done for her. The judge ruled that all Keith had to do was play a free concert for a school of the blind, and the resulting sentence also allowed things to cool enough for Keith to be granted permanent entry to the States with a green card. He would never be arrested again.

July: KEITH CLEANS UP

With his troubles mounting, Keith was making a determined effort to get clean, and was told by his lawyers that if he knew what was good for him – staying away from drugs and out of prison – then he should also stay away from Anita. Treated by Mick as a scapegoat for all of Keith's problems, it was the beginning of the end for the most important female in the Stones' circle.

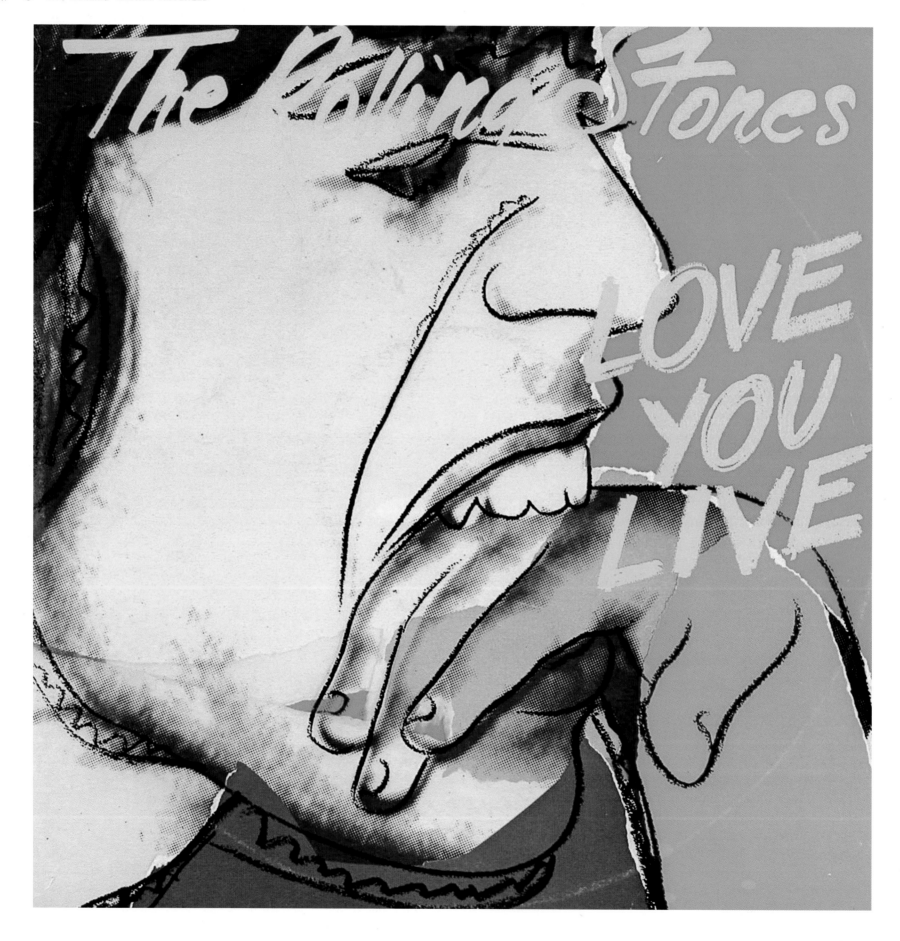

1978

September: LOVE YOU LIVE

With sleeve art by Andy Warhol – who was distraught when Jagger added some pencil scrawls to it – *Love You Live* was a double live album, with tracks taken from the 1975 TOTA, the night in Paris in 1976 when Keith was told of his son's death, and the club shows from Toronto in 1977. It was the final album on Rolling Stones Records, and it managed to go Top 10 in the UK and US.

May: 'MISS YOU'

Principally a Jagger song written for Jerry Hall, whom he'd met the previous year, and forming out of a jam with Billy Preston, 'Miss You' was the song that helped the Stones regain their commercial foothold in the 1970s, and also continued their overtly funk-and-disco-infused direction, building upon *Black And Blue*'s experiments. Hitting No. 3 in the UK and No. 1 in the States, it was not only built around a groove, but was also an unbelievably catchy song that would be the Stones' last monster single release. A near nine-minute version also exists, which was released as a 12-inch single for the disco/club market.

Some Girls
THE ROLLING STONES
Some Girls
Some Girls
PERMA-STYLED WASH -N- WEAR
Some Girls
READY FOR INSTANT WEAR
STYLE TST-79
Lies - lies you dirty Jezebel Why, why, why why don't you go to Hell?
MISS YOU $6.99
STYLE No PBF-79
$6.99
Pretty Baby FREEDOM
100% CAREFREE WASH & WEAR
Some girls give me jewelry
STYLE No CT-79
$6.99
Some Girls
Some GIRLS
RELAXED CURL
STYLE No TS-79
$6.99
GEORGIE Girl
TAPERED BACK $6.99
Some Girls
AFRO
100% CAREFREE WASH & WEAR
Synthetic Japanese Cordelon
Some Girls
INSTANT BEAUTY
PERMA-STYLED
100% WASH & WEAR
READY FOR INSTANT WEAR
6 in 1
FLIP UNDER or FLIP OUT
KOOL -N- ® LIGHT
Wash and Wear
French girls they want Cartier
LIGHT COOL AIRY–
Some Girls
Some Girls
Beast of Burden $7.99
STYLE No. DNY-89
Heavenly $7.99 BEAUTY
STYLE No. NC-89
$7.99
IMAGINATION
Far Away Eyes
Laughter, joy, and loneliness and sex and sex and sex and sex
FREEDOM WIG
SOFT RELAXED CURLS
Some girls give me children
100% Synthetic Japanese MODACRYLIC
COOL-CAPLESS Comfortable
PERMA-STYLED
Miracle Fibre
NEVER NEED SETTING
Some Girls
New Lovely You
KOOL -N- ® LIGHT
STYLE No. LIC-99
$8.99
STYLE No. LBC-99
Some Girls
Style No. MU-99
$8.99
CAPLESS SKIN-TOP BEAU CATCHER $8.99
SHATTERED
Synthetic Japanese MODACRYLIC
BOY-CUT Shorty
Black girls just wanta get ...
'When the Whip Comes Down' $8.99
WIZ-WIG
SUPER FREEDOM
Italian girls want cars
100% MIRACLE FIBRE
BEAUTIFUL YOU in a few seconds
BEAUTIFUL YOU in a few seconds
NEVER NEED SETTING
PERMA-STYLED
PART CENTER RIGHT or LEFT
FLIP UNDER or FLIP OUT
STYLE No. SK-109
100% WASH & WEAR
Some Girls
6 WIGS in ONE $9.99
STYLE No. SKGY-109
'Before They Make Me Run' Gypsy $9.99
DR. CORTIZONES' APPROVED
LIES Gypsy $9.99
STYLE No RS-109
$9.99
Skin-Crown
PERMANENT BUILT in HEIGHT
6 in 1
SOME GIRLS
Style No. SKPB-109
RESPECTABLE $9.99
$6.99
$6.99
$7.99
$7.99
$8.99
$8.99
$9.99
$9.99

June: SOME GIRLS

With punk – the antithesis to the touring behemoth the Stones had become (though many punks identified with Keith's 'up yours' attitude to authority) – having taken over rock's consciousness the previous year, the Stones' new album (for new label EMI) had to be something incredible. Their first with Ron Wood as a true full-time member, it traversed disco, punk and all-out rock; reinvigorated their fading fortunes, energies and now-aging audience; saved their career; and was actually their biggest-selling album. Interestingly, it marked the first time in 15 years that Keith would add the 's' back on to his surname, after Andrew Oldham suggested he drop it in 1963, to sound more like 'Cliff Richard'.

June: START OF AMERICAN TOUR

With Ian McLagan – keyboardist and old Face cohort of Ron's – in tow instead of Billy Preston, the Stones embarked on a gloomy tour of the US. Instead of celebrating their new-found commercial success, they lacked energy and had stripped down slightly from before; with Mick and Ron performing under the shadow of divorce, some lethargic renditions of old warhorse songs, a tired group in general, and a splitting of camps between Jagger (and Jerry Hall) and Keith. Ron was a fairly successful go-between, however, and with Keith finally off heroin for a tour, Ron even convinced him to allow Bill Wyman into his room to talk things over. The relationship between the two Stones had decayed drastically over the past 10 years.

September: 'BEAST OF BURDEN'

A US-only single, 'Beast Of Burden' was a Motown-influenced song from Keith that referenced his battles with heroin and begged Anita not to drag him down with her. The most emotional song on *Some Girls*, it was a perfect example of Ron and Keith's harmony through guitar playing – 'the ancient form of weaving', where neither took lead nor rhythm, but traded licks and grooves to create something almost transcendent and whole.

1980

June: EMOTIONAL RESCUE (ALBUM)

Taking their time to follow up *Some Girls*, *Emotional Rescue* was recorded beneath a barrage of insults flying back and forth from The Glimmer Twins – Keith was resentful of Mick's control of the band, and Mick wasn't interested in recording. Received as a slight let down after *Some Girls*, it was their first UK No. 1 album since *Goats Head Soup*, and incorporated a mix of styles, even if they were slightly tepid takes on things that could be found on *Some Girls*.

June: 'EMOTIONAL RESCUE' (SINGLE)

Reaching No. 9 in the UK and No. 3 in the US, releasing 'Emotional Rescue' as the lead single from their new album was one of the few things Mick and Keith could agree upon during the recording of the record. With Mick singing in falsetto, it was another one of the Stones' ballad lead-single releases.

1981

March: SUCKING IN THE SEVENTIES

Released as a follow-up to their 1974 compilation *Made In The Shade*, *Sucking In The Seventies* was a perfunctory 1975-onwards collection of songs, including 'Everything Is Turning To Gold' (the B-side to 'Shattered'); 'If I Was A Dancer Pt. 2' (which picked up from where *Emotional Rescue*'s title track left off); and a live version of 'When The Whip Comes Down', originally released on *Some Girls*.

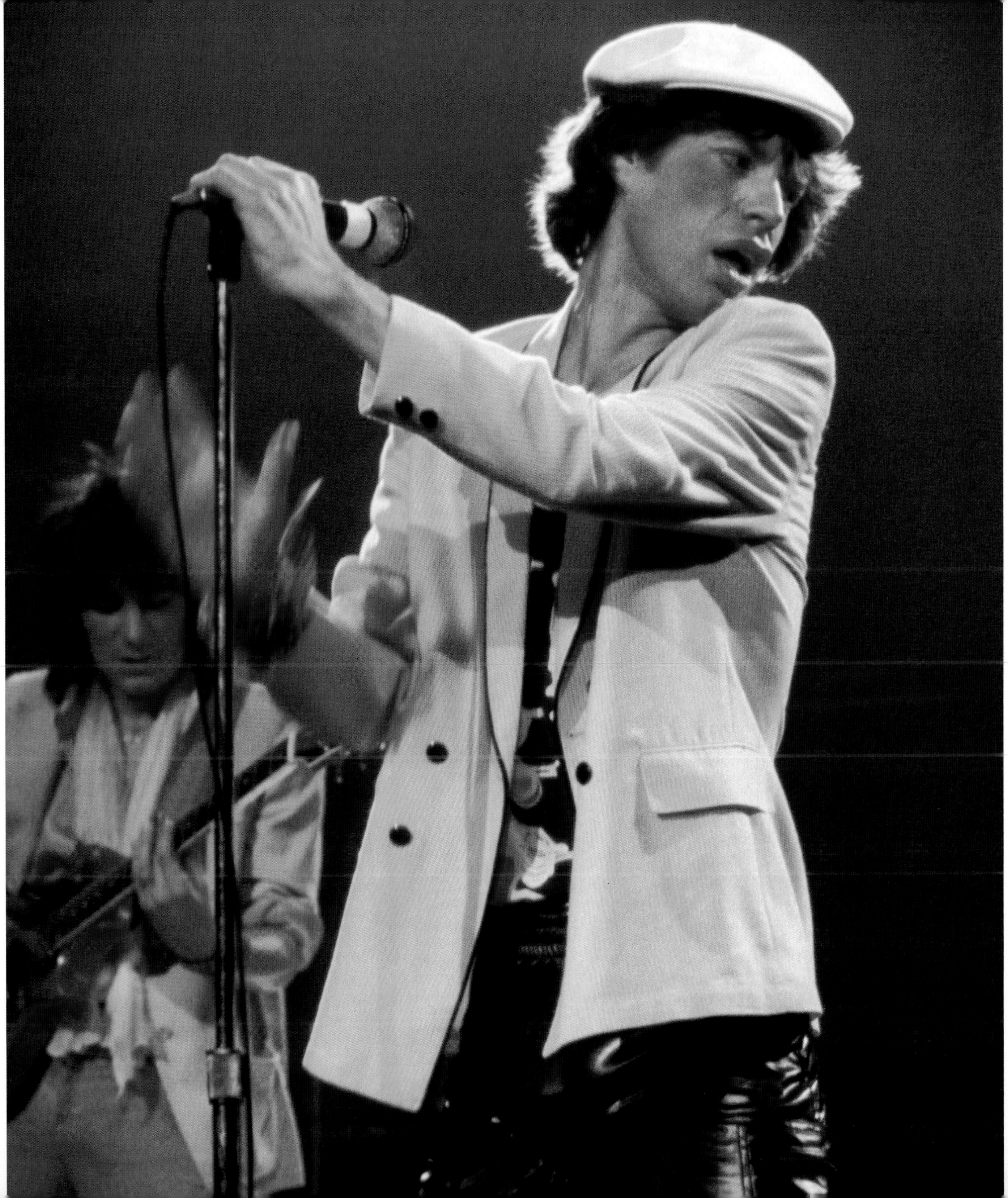

August: 'START ME UP'

One of the group's most infectious riffs, and forthcoming album opener, 'Start Me Up' actually dated back to the 1977 *Some Girls* sessions, where it was written as a reggae song. After overdubbing guitars on to the one 'rock' take they recorded in 1977, Keith nixed the idea of it appearing even on *Emotional Rescue*, as he was worried that he had written the riff from another song. A mindless piece of rock'n'roll about a woman who can make dead men reach orgasm, it remains one of the group's last memorable singles, even though it reached Nos. 2 and 7 in the US and UK respectively.

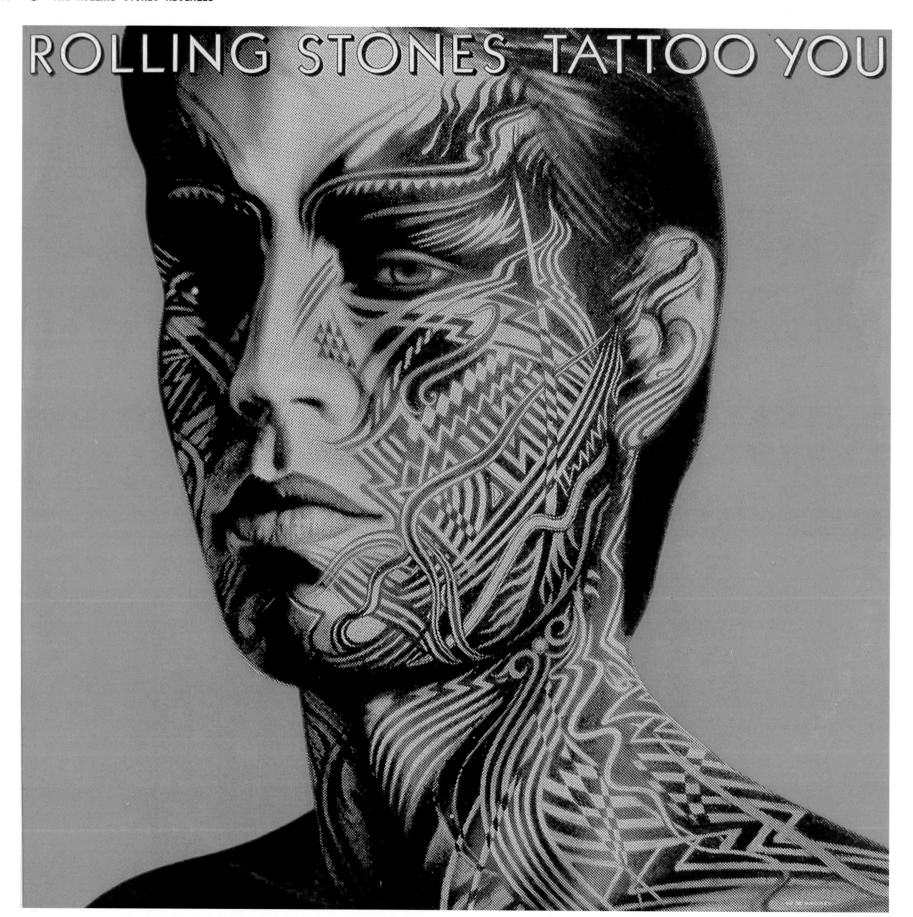

August: TATTOO YOU

Whereas a few albums from the last decade saw riffs looking for songs, in the early 1980s the Stones were looking for anything. Running out of steam, *Tattoo You* (originally intended to be just called *Tattoo*) was mostly assembled from ideas and outtakes stretching back to *Goats Head Soup* ('Tops', 1972) and even, some claim, 1970's *Sticky Fingers* sessions ('Waiting On A Friend'). Mostly mid- to late-1970s ideas and fragments, it nevertheless became the Stones' last US No. 1 album.

September: START OF NORTH AMERICAN TOUR

Hardly enamoured with the idea of touring, Jagger, who had been in firm training as the group's *de facto* leader for some time, approached it now as more of a business chore, carrying calculators and diaries around during US shows, selling the film rights to live recordings, and trying to implement a no-drugs policy. Keith and Ron complained about him as 'Brenda' behind his back, while Ron was fast descending into the state that Keith had been escaping from. Despite internal hatreds, it was a fairly slick show and one of the first tours to see the Stones' original fans aging with them, and a new generation of fans coming along as well.

THE ROLLING STONES 1982-1999

1982-99

Like punk had never happened, the Stones continued into the 1980s as a juggernaut rock act. But like many 1960s and 1970s successes (Bob Dylan, David Bowie), they struggled to fit into a decade where technology was changing, music was changing and bands could be made or broken on the strength of a promotional video for MTV.

Music had become a business, and no one understood this more than Jagger, who allowed 'Start Me Up' to be used on a Microsoft Windows advert. While Keith remained the beating heart of the group, holding the Stones together, at the same time as trying to assume a more prominent role in the wake of kicking his heroin addiction, Jagger seemed to lose more and more interest in group duties, focusing on a solo career that would almost cause the Stones to implode. Infighting (and out-fighting, as Mick and Keith exchanged insults in the press) characterized the Stones for the 1980s, as its two chief songwriters embarked on World War Three.

Patching up somewhat for the 1990s (though without Bill Wyman, who left officially in 1993), Mick was still very much leading the band towards the *zeitgeist*, staging extravagant stadium tours popularized by the likes of U2 and Michael Jackson – heavy on the effects, low on the audience connection. And though they would release their best album in 20 years, 1997's *Bridges To Babylon*, the end of the decade saw the Stones disappear for a few years, having become more of a Las Vegas-style hits act.

1982

June: STILL LIFE (AMERICAN CONCERT 1981)

Recorded during the group's US *Tattoo You* tour the previous year, *Still Life* was released on 1 June, in time to coincide with their European tour, which started on 2 June. Entering the Top 5 US and UK charts, it wasn't as well received by the press, who criticized it for being too slick, and having none of the Stones' rough edges.

1983

August: SIGN WITH CBS

With Atlantic disinterested in signing the Stones for the tens of millions they wanted, they signed with CBS for £28 million (allegedly double the amount offered by the next label in line), for four new albums and the rights to their back catalogue up to 1971. Part of the deal was also a guarantee that Jagger would deliver the label a solo album.

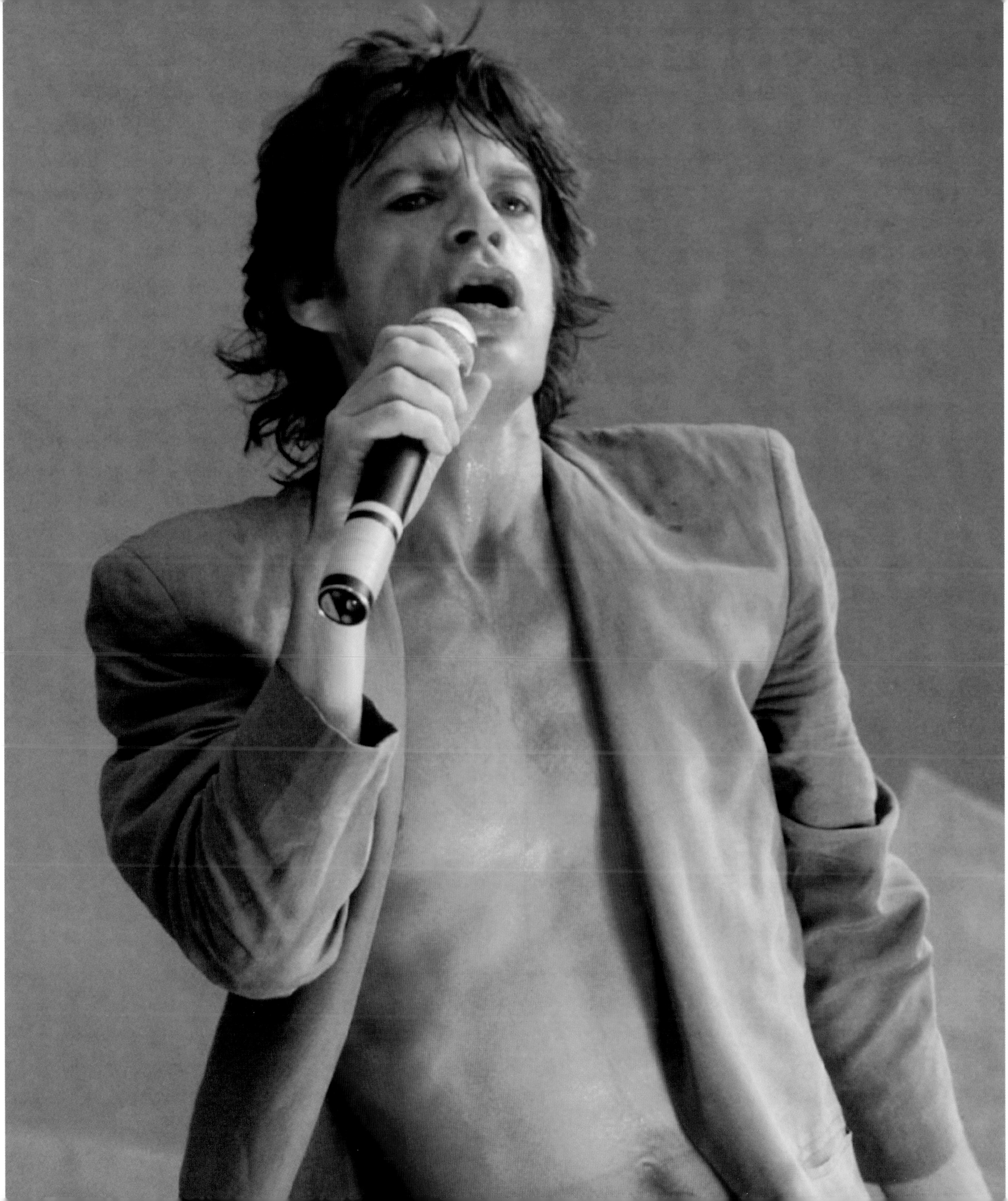

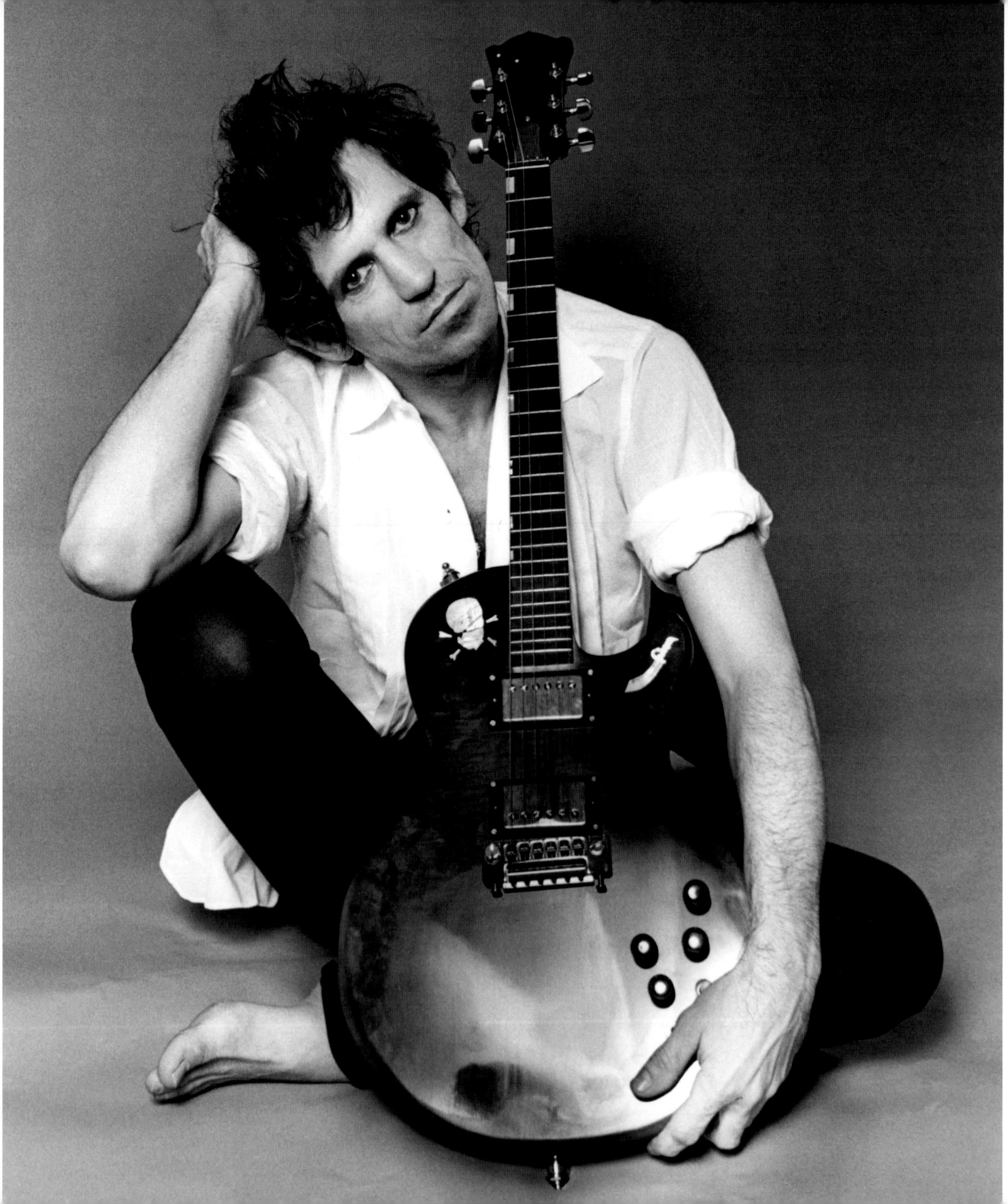

November: UNDERCOVER

The air was thick with tension during the recording of *Undercover*, their last original album for Rolling Stones Records. Keith, now looking to reclaim an active role in the group, often turned up in the studio wearing a cape and waving a sword-like stick, but didn't stick around for all of the final mixing sessions. Image-conscious Jagger wanted the group to stay up with current trends, and Richards was more interested in sticking with their rock'n'roll roots – an argument that would continue into the next decade, and which became an entry point into further fighting between the two. *Undercover* is viewed by many as the final release before the Stones' power weakened for good, and the last album to try anything different and progressive.

November: 'UNDERCOVER OF THE NIGHT'

'Undercover Of The Night' had a violent promotional video that caused controversy. Mick intended for it to keep the group current and introduce them to the MTV generation. Following a sketchy storyline and with partially politicized impressions of inner-city violence in the US, the single reached No. 11 in the UK and No. 9 in the US.

December: PATTI HANSON

Keith met Patti Hanson at his birthday party in 1979 and quickly began to date her. Four years later to the day they were married, with Keith saying, 'I know I couldn't have beaten heroin without Patti. I ain't letting that bitch go!' With Mick as best man, the wedding would see Keith enter a period of domestic bliss.

1984

July: REWIND (1971–1984)

Repeating a lot of tracks from previous compilations, *Rewind (1971–1984)* was a retrospective of the last 13 years. It marked the end of EMI's distribution of Rolling Stones Records in the UK (Warner Bros. in the US), mostly taking in the singles, and being the first compilation since 1969's *Through The Past, Darkly (Big Hits, Volume 2)* to feature different UK and US tracklistings, in order to appeal to the different markets.

1985

February: JAGGER RELEASES SHE'S THE BOSS

 The first of four solo albums (the others being *Primitive Cool*, 1987; *Wandering Spirit*, 1993; and *Goddess In The Doorway*, 2001), *She's The Boss* was Jagger stretching out and exploring the contemporary pop direction he wanted the Stones to pursue. Releasing it as the first 'Stones' record for CBS was the final straw for Keith. He was infuriated with Jagger's disinterest in the band, envisioned future conflicts between solo and group interests, and threatened to slit Mick's throat if he toured with another band. Lukewarmly received by critics, *She's The Boss*'s greatest legacy was that it set the Stones on course for what would be their mid-1980s breakdown (Keith would later refer to it as World War Three), with The Glimmer Twins playing out their bitter arguments publicly.

July: LiVE AiD

Evidence of the fractured state the band was in, Jagger would perform 'Just Another Night' and 'Miss You' solo at Live Aid on 13 July, with help then arriving from Tina Turner (who had taught Mick to dance when she was an Ikette on tour with the Stones in 1966), for 'State Of Shock' (a recent hit single he recorded with The Jackson Five) and 'It's Only Rock'n'Roll'. Ron and Keith would play behind Dylan for his finale to the day's event, with terrible and under-rehearsed performances of three Dylan originals, 'Ballad Of Hollis Brown', 'When The Ship Comes In' and 'Blowin' In The Wind'.

December: IAN 'STU' STEWART DiES

One of the Stones' founding band members, though left out of the 'official' group line-up at Andrew Oldham's behest because he didn't look the part, Ian 'Stu' Stewart died of a heart attack at the age of 47 on 12 December. Widely acknowledged as being the glue that kept the Stones together ('It was Stu's band really,' Keith would say shortly after), the Stones were traumatized for months, unable to see a clear way forward. On 28 February, billed as 'Rocket '86', they played a private tribute show for Stewart at London's 100 Club – an appearance that also served to disprove rumours that the Stones were splitting.

1986

March: 'HARLEM SHUFFLE'

In a period that saw *The Blues Brothers* make white-folks-singing-black-music popular, the Stones had been more than 20 years ahead of their time; and Bob & Earl's soul classic, 'Harlem Shuffle' was a song that Keith had wanted to get Mick to cover for years. When they finally did, Jagger entered the studio, did his vocal in two takes, and left, leaving Bobby Womack and Tom Waits to fill out backing vocals later. With a promo video that mixed live action with animation (courtesy of future *Ren & Stimpy* animator, John Kricfalusi), the single went to No. 5 in the US, and only No. 13 in the UK.

March: DIRTY WORK

Recorded while Jagger and Keith were at their most vitriolic (Keith's songs like 'Fight', 'Had It With You' and 'One Hit (To The Body)' would say it all; Jagger made it clear that he was more interested in promoting his own album instead of recording with the Stones), *Dirty Work* was dedicated to Ian Stewart. Intended to be a return to rock roots, with co-production from The Glimmer Twins and legendary producer Steve Lillywhite, its embarrassing sleeve boasted the group in day-glo suits – and the music wasn't much better. There were no real hits, the group weren't functioning together at all, and *Dirty Work* fast became the worst Stones album ever.

DIRTY WORK

ROLLING STONES

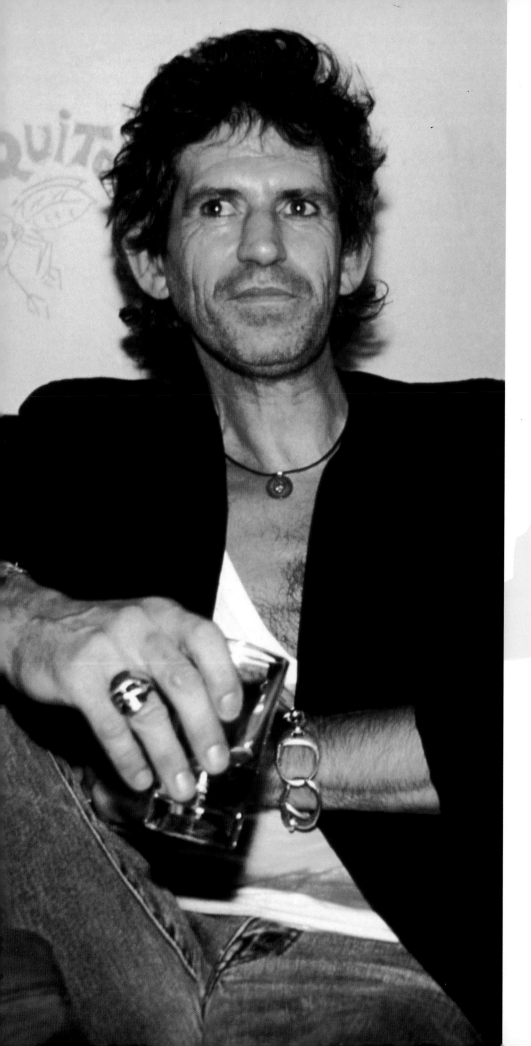

1988

October: RICHARDS RELEASES TALK IS CHEAP

Much better received than Jagger's own solo output – a victory for the man whose band was falling apart in front of him – *Talk Is Cheap* was almost forced upon Richards, who couldn't rest, but was in creative deadlock with the Stones. Forming his band, The X-Pensive Winos, from out of the house band he assembled for the 1987 Chuck Berry documentary *Hail! Hail! Rock'n'Roll*, Richards' solo album was praised as the best Stones record since *Exile* by some fans, and certainly the only promise of their being any spark in future Stones releases, with Richards at his most relaxed and creative of the decade.

1989

January: KEITH AND MICK MEET IN BARBADOS

Missing in action for almost three years, the Stones' future was uncertain. The new wave of rock groups like Guns N' Roses (Axl Rose pictured on the right) had built themselves on the Stones' template, but the forefathers were nowhere to be seen. In mid-January, Keith flew out to Mick in Barbados to discuss the future of the band and the possibility of writing songs again. Allegedly, he told his wife that he'd be home in either two days or two weeks. When she'd not heard from him after a few days, Patti called him to ask, 'Two weeks, then?' 'Happily, yes,' Keith replied, having been working on new songs with Mick almost since they met.

January: INDUCTED TO ROCK'N'ROLL HALL OF FAME

Six days after reconvening with Mick, the pair arrived in New York on 18 January to be inducted to the Rock'n'Roll Hall Of Fame by Pete Townshend. It was their first public appearance together since 1986, though the group didn't play. Bill refused to attend, saying that the honours were too little too late, and even Mick and Keith were slightly worried that the recognition would pigeonhole them as 1960s has-beens. When presenting the award, Townshend encouraged, 'Whatever you do, don't try to grow old gracefully. It wouldn't suit you.'

June: MANDY SMITH

After a secret registrar church wedding on 2 June (which further suggested that Bill's interests were not with the band), three days later Bill invited everyone else (who begrudgingly attended) to a church wedding between his 53-year-old self and the now 19-year-old Mandy Smith – the girl he'd been having an affair with since she was 13. That same month he opened a rock memorabilia burger restaurant, Sticky Fingers, without his bandmates' permission – something which added to the Stones' general annoyance with Wyman, and resulted in more severing of ties.

August: 'MIXED EMOTIONS'

Recounting the will-they-won't-they feeling behind the group's keeping together, 'Mixed Emotions' was one of the earliest songs Jagger and Richards worked on in Barbados, and reflected the resentment and bitterness that bubbled under the surface during recordings for the new album. Only reaching No. 36 in the UK charts, it fared better in the States, rising to No. 5.

August: STEEL WHEELS

Mick and Keith having buried the hatchet, *Steel Wheels* at least kept the band on the rails, and was the awkward commercial comeback the Stones needed, reaching No. 1 in America and No. 2 in the UK. Bridging the two songwriting camps (Ron and Keith's more emotion-led playing; Mick's more aesthetically angled songs) was Charlie, who drove the band along and settled any disagreements that could lead to argument – though working so fast, the group didn't have much time to fall out. It was an attempt to return to a true Stones rock basis, and would also be Bill Wyman's last studio album with the group.

ROLLING STONES STEEL WHEELS

August: STEEL WHEELS TOUR STARTS

Conceived by Mick as celebrating the dawn of the digital age, the *Steel Wheels* live shows cost $4 million to put together, with the scaffold-designed set resembling a decaying industrial world. The 62 US dates saw recorded samples, synthesizers and a full brass section added to the stage show, which covered a mix of classics and new songs across a 28-song set that tried to highlight every period of the group's career.

1990

February: FIRST CONCERT IN JAPAN

Playing their first ever Japanese tour dates, the Stones sold out
10 dates at the Tokyo Dome, a venue more accustomed to hosting
baseball matches. Mark Fisher, London architect and designer of the
stage set, came over to re-jig the cumbersome Steel Wheels setup,
which would result in the Urban Jungle design.

May: URBAN JUNGLE TOUR OF EUROPE

Stripping down from the Steel Wheels stage set, the Urban Jungle design was easier to move around on the 45 European dates it was used. Though the actual shows would remain similar set-list wise, there was more reliance on jokey stage props reminiscent of the 1975 Tour Of The Americas. During 'Street Fighting Man', rehearsed as a big production number, four large, toothy blow-up dogs – complete with erections – would be unleashed, with one of them eating Jagger at the end of the song.

September: JERRY HALL

After years of prodding and goading, Mick finally married Jerry Hall in the South Pacific. The Texan supermodel had actually been Bryan Ferry's girlfriend when she met Mick in 1977, but it didn't take long for Mick to take advantage of Ferry's touring absences and work his way into Hall's heart. The marriage would ultimately fail quite publicly nine years later, leading Hall to say, 'Mick's a wonderful man, and a terrible husband.'

1991

April: FLASHPOINT

Recorded across the *Steel Wheels/Urban Jungle* tour, and their last album for CBS, *Flashpoint* was unique for the Stones' live albums in that it included two exclusive new studio tracks, 'Highwire' (inspired by the First Gulf War) and 'Sex Drive'. Wyman played on both of these, but he refused to appear in the 'Highwire' promotional video, making the songs his last for the group – though he wouldn't officially retire until 1993. Taking in a lot of hits, and some more obscurer catalogue songs like 'Factory Girl', *Flashpoint* was a fair reflection of the Stones' live shows as they were recorded.

November: SIGN WITH VIRGIN RECORDS

Come the end of their CBS deal, the label had been sold to Sony, and its charismatic head, Walter Yentikoff, no longer worked there. Though the rumour was that Richard Branson wanted to sign the Stones to make his Virgin record label more attractive for selling on himself, Mick was interested in signing with the label, and the Stones received a rumoured $45 million for a three-album deal. Wyman refused to sign the contract, so its terms and conditions allowed him a year to think about it. Within four months, Branson sold the label and used the money to start Virgin Air.

1992

TIME OUT

1992 was a sparse year for the group, who took some time out from being 'the Stones'. Mick worked on his third solo project, *Wandering Spirit*, with Rick Rubin; Keith reconvened with The X-Pensive Winos for his second solo album, *Main Offender*, and rumours spread that Bill Wyman had quit the band, deciding that rock no longer had a place in a world where rap, grunge and the fledgling Britpop movement were beginning to rule the airwaves.

1993

January: BILL WYMAN QUITS

Appearing live on *London Tonight*, Bill Wyman officially stated what many had thought – or at least felt – for more than a year and a half: he was quitting The Rolling Stones. Having recently settled a divorce with Mandy for nearly $1 million, he wanted to put his past behind him. Ron joked that he understood, because Bill was 'two thousand years old', and Jagger claimed not to be fazed. Even Keith, then on tour promoting his solo album, seemed to be more annoyed that they'd have to find a new bass player – a chore which was ultimately left up to Charlie, who would pick one-time Miles Davis bass player, Darryl Jones, to go on tour and play in the studio with them, though not join the group officially.

1994

June: SONGWRITERS' HALL OF FAME

With over 200 of their own songs having been written and released up to this point – with presumably hundreds more that never saw the light of day – Mick and Keith were inducted to the Songwriters' Hall Of Fame on 2 June 1993.

July: VOODOO LOUNGE

Voodoo Lounge, their first album in five years (and ending the longest Stones absence), was the group's first release for Virgin, and their first UK chart-topper since 1980's *Emotional Rescue*. Like its predecessor, *Steel Wheels*, *Voodoo Lounge* was designed to get back to classic, stripped-down rock, and had a rawer, more authentic feel than *Wheels*. Trying to play on their past devilish imagery with the sleeve, the record wasn't great, and even Mick's opinion seemed muted when he told *Rolling Stone* magazine, 'The ballads are rather nice … and then the rock'n'roll numbers sound enthusiastic'. Perhaps the most progressive aspect of the release was the tie-in *Voodoo Lounge* CD-ROM interactive computer game released the following year.

August: START OF VOODOO LOUNGE TOUR

Another $4-million stage set (this time paid for by a brewery, making *Voodoo Lounge* the world's first sponsored tour) accompanied the Stones on their worldwide *Voodoo Lounge* tour, which set a record at grossing around $140 million and lasted until August 1995. With stage and lighting effects taken from recent megatours by Michael Jackson and U2, the concept was again technological, as the Stones played in front of a huge Jumbotron screen, riding the 'Information Highway' to 'Wired City', surrounded by a cobra-shaped tower, banks of light and pyrotechnics, making the set resemble something of a metal volcano. To re-learn their old songs, the group listened to their albums' CD re-issues, with Mick cribbing lyrics from an old Stones songbook.

November: INTERNET CONCERT

Allegedly motivated to make one of their *Voodoo Lounge* shows a webcast because it was feared that Aerosmith might beat them to it, the Stones became the first *mainstream* rock band to webcast one of their shows when they played the Cotton Bowl in Dallas, Texas on 18 November. Not actually the first band to do so, however, the Stones were livid when group Severe Tire Damage performed an 'opening act' webcast 30 minutes before the Stones were due to go onstage, although they'd even been there before, in June 1993, as part of a scientific experiment in Australia.

1995

November: STRIPPED

With the *Voodoo Lounge* tour receiving some criticism for being too much of a spectacle, and Mick disappointed that the *Voodoo Lounge* songs didn't come off as well live, the Stones played some 'Stripped' club shows as a way to underplay their previous extravagances. From these came the basis of the *Stripped* live album. These were added to with some acoustic renditions of older songs, which were recorded live-in-the-studio in Japan. With bonus CD-ROM interviews and behind-the-scenes footage, the album was received by critics as one of their best live releases, and reached No. 9 in the States.

1997

September: BRIDGES TO BABYLON

A genuine return to some sort of form, and their best since *Some Girls*, *Bridges To Babylon* was again the product of a band working as two different factions, but at least getting it to sound right. Even so, the band weren't speaking by the end of the recording, and throughout Mick was experimenting with hip-hop producers The Dust Brothers – who had worked with Beck and The Beastie Boys – while Keith stuck with *Voodoo Lounge* producer Don Was. Still, it was the most passionate recording the group had made in two decades, though lead single 'Anybody Seen My Baby?' would have to be given a last-minute co-writing credit, after Richards' daughter Angela noticed its resemblance to kd lang's 'Constant Craving'.

September: BRIDGES TO BABYLON TOUR

Arguably, the Stones were now more a live draw than an exciting albums' band, and the *Bridges To Babylon* shows would see them tour the world for a year. Again influenced by modern stage technology, the set had a bridge that stretched out over the audience, leading the group to a small, raised platform where they would play a club-style set. Every night saw internet users pick one song for the setlist, which itself included plenty of crowd pleasers. Though highly successful, this was the tour that saw the Stones settle into being more of a rolling Vegas 'hits' act, as opposed to a vital band of the times.

1998

November: NO SECURITY

Not a successful seller by any means (No. 67 UK; No. 34 US), *No Security* was recorded on the *Bridges To Babylon* tour and released to appease a record company that wanted the overblown live stadium album. Compiled of songs that hadn't seen a live album release before – or at least not for a long time – most of the recordings were stadium singalongs from *Babylon*'s Amsterdam shows. The record was a sales disaster, and even Mick claimed to have only heard it once.

1999

January: START OF NO SECURITY TOUR

With clothes company Tommy Hilfiger sponsoring, the Stones' arena tour in support of *No Security* began in January 1999, as Jerry Hall was filing for a divorce with Mick. Like a mini-version of their previous stadium tours, *No Security* shows were treated as homecoming crowd pleasers from start to finish, with the Stones opening each night by showing a film of themselves walking to the stage from their dressing rooms – something akin to the heroism of slow-motion movies clips of astronauts walking to the launch pad.

May: EUROPEAN BRIDGES TO BABYLON TOUR

The Stones went out on an heroic – if not creative – high, playing 11 postponed European *Bridges To Babylon* shows at outdoor stadiums, just before disappearing again. With the same sort of crowd-pleasing approach the *No Security* shows had, audience reaction was good (despite a listless Wembley Stadium appearance), and the general feeling was clear: the Stones were old rock masters with nothing more to prove; just seeing them was good enough. And by the time the tour ended, the Stones had taken $300 million.

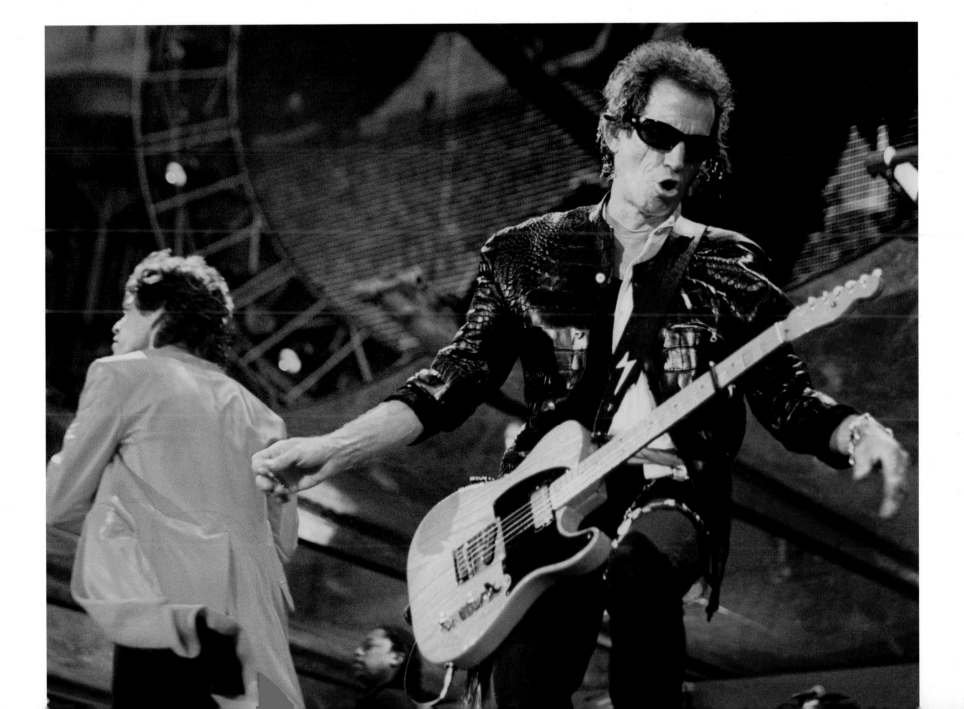

2000–PRESENT

If the Stones ended the 1990s with a slightly dubious future ahead of them, the Noughties saw critics and the public alike ready and willing to embrace them again.

With the career-spanning *Forty Licks* compilation in the shops, fans old and new were encouraged to rediscover the Stones' past glories, and a 2002/03 worldwide tour saw them continue to churn out the hits, but to ecstatic audiences and a critical reception that, though conceding the Stones had perhaps written their best, accepted that, with a legacy such as theirs, it no longer mattered.

Survivors of what, to many, is rock's Golden Age, the Stones' 2005 album *A Bigger Bang* was *fêted* by many and helped them to continue riding high. It was just one aspect of their success in the Noughties, a decade that saw them play to their largest-ever audience. Mick Jagger, once a public enemy who spent time at Her Majesty's Pleasure, received a knighthood in 2003; and after a shock diagnosis of throat cancer in 2004, Charlie Watts had fully recovered by February 2005; while Ron Wood has had his own successes, apparently managing to keep his alcohol problems under control since the *Licks* tour ended in 2003.

Not one without misadventure, however, perhaps it's Keith Richards who best symbolizes where the Stones are at this point in their career, as they continue to tour the world into 2007. Having received emergency brain surgery to remove a blood clot after falling out of a tree in May 2006, Richards continues to live up to his motto: 'It's good to be here. It's good to be anywhere!'

ROLLING STONES
FORTY LICKS

2002

September:
FORTY LICKS RELEASED; FORTY LICKS TOUR

Forty Licks was a 2-CD compilation released to large fanfare, being the Stones' first entire career-spanning compilation to cover both their Decca and self-owned post-1970 recordings. The *Forty Licks* tour took off almost instantly in the same month. Trying to reconnect with their audience and just focus on the music, the Stones intended for it to be 'Rolling Stones On The Road: World Tour 2002/2003 Arena/Stadium/ Club', with no special-effects laden sets, just a load of classic songs. The 'Arena/Stadium/Club' concept would see them play different venues of differing sizes in each area they visited (in London they played Twickenham Stadium, Wembley Arena and London's Astoria), with radically differing setlists each night that drew great excitement from fans eager to catch rare live outings of songs many thought the Stones wouldn't play again. The tour also resulted in its own live *Forty Licks* compilation, and the *Four Flicks* 4-DVD box set.

November: APPEARANCE ON THE SIMPSONS

Following in a long line of celebrities – rock stars and otherwise – appearing on *The Simpsons*, Mick and Keith were star guests of series 14, episode two ('How I Spent My Strummer Vacation'). Originally aired on 10 November 2002, they played themselves as owners of a rock'n'roll fantasy camp. Caught blaming his family for the way his life has gone, Homer is sent to the camp in order to live his rock'n'roll dreams. Come the end, Homer becomes the Stones' roadie (though he thinks he's invited on tour as the star of the show). The episode also featured Lenny Kravitz, Tom Petty and Elvis Costello as teachers at the camp.

2003

July: SARS BENEFIT CONCERT, TORONTO

Taking a month to plan (the show was announced while Toronto was still under health warning from the World Trade Organization), the Stones staged and headlined a benefit concert for Toronto, Canada, quite often called 'Toronto Rocks' or 'SARSapalooza'. Playing Downsview Park to 450,000–500,000 people, the show helped raise financial aid and spirits for a city devastated by the SARS (Sever Acute Respiratory Syndrome) epidemic that had hit Toronto in 2003.

November: FIRST CONCERT IN HONG KONG

Initially pulled from the Harbour Fest bill after delays in signing a contract, the Stones played their first ever shows in Hong Kong at the Tamar festival site, as part of another SARS benefit concert. Performing on 7 and 9 November, the shows also replaced those cancelled earlier in the year when the epidemic broke.

December: SiR MiCK JAGGER

As of 12 December 2003, Mick Jagger would legally be Sir Mick Jagger, having received a knighthood for his 'services to popular music'. Many questioned whether someone with a past that included drug run-ins with the law could rightfully be knighted. More still wondered why Keith wasn't also bestowed with the honour. Perhaps the monarchy had anticipated his response to Mick's award. He told the *Independent*, 'It's not what the Stones is about, is it? I don't want to step out on stage with someone wearing a f***ing coronet and sporting the old ermine. I told Mick, it's a f***ing paltry honour.'

2004

June: CHARLIE WATTS

The backbone of the Stones' sound, and the only member not to have any overtly publicized drug mishaps (though he allegedly dabbled with heroin in the 1980s), Charlie Watts was diagnosed with throat cancer in June 2004, at the age of 63. Attending radiotherapy sessions, many people's favourite Stone and jazz musician in his own right, made a full recovery by February 2005, and instantly went to work on the Stones' next album.

2005

August: START OF A BIGGER BANG TOUR

Kicking off their *A Bigger Bang* tour with a warm-up show in Toronto's 1,000-capacity Phoenix Concert Theatre, the band started a year-long, worldwide tour, playing a mix of classics and songs from their *A Bigger Bang* album to arena and stadium shows. They even played at the half-time of Superbowl XL, and by the end of 2006 the Stones had performed over 100 shows in support of *A Bigger Bang*, even staging the largest tour run in US history.

September: A BIGGER BANG RELEASED

Their first full-length release of original material since 1997's *Bridges To Babylon*, *A Bigger Bang* received mostly strong reviews and was a return to the group's no-frills rock side that would find a home in the contemporary mid-Noughties scene spearheaded by the likes of The White Stripes. Although not a huge unit-shifter, the lead single, 'Streets Of Love', made it to No. 15 UK, and the album would peak at No. 2 UK and No. 3 US. With very little input from outside musicians, *A Bigger Bang* was recorded at Mick's home in France, and was certainly evidence of a revitalized unit. They even offered flashes of their old controversy with 'Sweet Neo Con', an attack on America's neoconservatism. It was further proof of their continuing popularity, even if they were no longer competing with contemporary pop artists.

2006

February: COPACABANA BEACH

On Copacabana Beach, Rio de Janeiro, Brazil, the Stones played to their largest-ever audience, a free concert held on 18 February 2006. The crowd was estimated at 1,500,000, and was one of the largest free concerts in history to date.

April: FIRST CHINESE CONCERT

On 8 April, the Stones played in Shanghai, the first time they would ever perform in China, after shows planned for 2003 were cancelled due to the breakout of SARS. With concern over their suggestive lyrics, the authorities ordered them not to play 'Brown Sugar', 'Honky Tonk Women', 'Beast Of Burden' and 'Let's Spend The Night Together'.

May: RICHARDS' ACCIDENT

Forcing a postponement of the *A Bigger Bang* tour, Keith Richards underwent brain surgery in May after falling out of a tree in late April. While on holiday in Fiji during a month's break from the tour, Keith was reportedly climbing the tree with Ronnie when he fell out. After initially seeming OK, the fall became more serious than he thought when, in early May, he had to undergo surgery in a New Zealand hospital, in order to treat a blood clot on the brain.

July: EUROPEAN LEG OF A BIGGER BANG TOUR

After completely recovering from his brain operation, Keith and the band were ready to continue their *A Bigger Bang* tour in Europe, launching it with a press conference in Milan, where Keith assured the journalists that he was back to strength, saying 'I feel totally normal, whatever that means.... If you saw the tree, you'd realize the joke.'

The whole event was strangely reminiscent of a defensive quote he'd given for some of the *Voodoo Lounge* shows 11 years before: 'We're the only band to take it this far. And if you see us trip and fall, you'll know that's how far it can go.'

The postponed European shows were rescheduled for 2007.

INDEX